BUDDHISM:
The Plain Facts

by Robert Mann & Rose Youd
BUDDHIST CHARACTER ANALYSIS

by Robert Mann
BUDDHISM IN A FOREIGN LAND

BUDDHISM:
The Plain Facts

Robert Mann & Rose Youd

AUKANA

BRADFORD ON AVON

First published 1998
Reprinted 1999, 2000, 2004

Aukana Trust
9 Masons Lane
Bradford on Avon
Wiltshire
BA15 1QN
England

e-mail: info@aukana.org.uk
www.aukana.org.uk
Telephone: (01225) 866821
International: +44 1225 866821

Typeset in Bembo 11/13.5 by LP&TS Publishing, Somerton
Printed in Great Britain by The Cromwell Press, Trowbridge

Cover printed by Devenish & Co, Bath
Cover photograph © Travellerseye Ltd/Vicki Couchman 1996
(from 'A Trail of Visions - Route 1 India, Sri Lanka, Thailand, Sumatra')

A catalogue record for this book is available from the British Library

ISBN 0-9511769-7-8

CONTENTS

Why Follow The Path?

Why follow the path? Because, in the last analysis, things aren't good enough.

All of us want to be happy. Most of us, at least in our earlier years, assume that happiness **can** be found in the world. We believe that given enough money, the right relationships, a satisfying career we could be happy, permanently happy.

With the disappointments that inevitably come our way, our optimism begins to wear thin. However much money we have, we could always do with more ... Our relationships never really match up to our ideals ... Work is always either too challenging or not challenging enough.

Sometimes, of course, there are moments when everything is going well and there is nothing we would want to change - but even these moments are flawed. The better life seems, the more we've got to lose. Happiness is a fragile state. Sooner or later, the realisation dawns that even the most perfect moment fades.

But many of us have a remarkable facility for burying such insights. Time and time again we refuse to pay attention to our growing sense of disillusionment and we redouble our efforts to find satisfaction in money, relationships, work, whatever. However hard we try, however enthusiastically we throw ourselves into the quest for happiness, however avidly we pretend to ourselves that everything is OK really, it is not long before discontent resurfaces.

In the end, having tried just about everything we can think of, we are forced to start looking beyond our usual horizons.

In many cases, it is simply the relentless accumulation of minor frustrations that provides the impetus for finding a spiritual path. Alternatively, the motivation may be some sudden trauma - a diagnosis of terminal illness, the loss of a job, the break-up of a relationship; a short sharp shock that clearly reveals that life is not what we would like it to be.

In short, it is because of the existence of pain, disappointment, frustration that we look for a way out.

Many paths claim to lead to permanent happiness. Some live up to their promise - some may only provide temporary relief - others don't work at all.

The Buddha said, quite simply, that **his** way leads to enlightenment, to the total eradication of every aspect of distress.

Buddhism

In the two and a half millennia that have passed since the Buddha first taught, Buddhism has spread across the globe. It has divided and sub-divided into different schools and sects, each taking on a distinct cultural identity. Today, Buddhism can stand for Theravada Buddhism, Zen Buddhism, Tibetan Buddhism, Mahayana Buddhism ... Every variation has its own history, its own traditions, its own scriptures.

Buddhism, it might seem, is a highly complicated proposition.

But however esoteric or intricate the various philosophies and religious forms of Buddhism might appear, the fundamental teaching is simplicity itself. For all schools of Buddhism share this central tenet: that there is an effective path to freedom, to the complete elimination of all distress and unhappiness.

That the path works is not something to be taken on trust. It is something that anyone who is prepared to put it into practice can find out for themselves. The Buddha described his teaching as 'a come-and-see thing'. He wasn't teaching a philosophical theory but a practical way to true happiness.

The Four Noble Truths:
Suffering

The whole of the Buddha's teaching - the Dhamma - can be summarised in four concise statements known as the noble truths.

The first truth confirms our perception that there is a problem. It acknowledges frustration, anguish, discontent as facts of life. As the Buddha said, 'There is suffering'. This unequivocal statement is the starting-point of the whole of the teaching.

The term the Buddha used which is normally translated as 'suffering' is *dukkha*★. Suffering is in some ways a misleading translation because, although *dukkha* certainly does mean anguish, distress, misery, it also means a lot more.

Suffering can be acute - the anguish felt, for example, at the death of somebody close or at the failure of a relationship. More commonly, it is less traumatic - maybe a general sense of loneliness and isolation, or a sense of the futility of existence. Losing the car keys, having to relate to a boring neighbour, having to go in to work after the weekend - these are all *dukkha*.

★ *Dukkha* is a Pali word, Pali being the ancient Indian language in which the teachings were first recorded.

Experiencing things we don't want to experience is *dukkha* - not experiencing the things we do want to experience is also *dukkha*.

The Buddha did not deny, however, that happiness can be found in the world. This is one of the most commonly misunderstood ideas in Buddhism. Many jump to the conclusion that with the first noble truth the Buddha was painting a picture of life that was relentlessly pessimistic.

Clearly there is happiness in the world. Not only was this acknowledged by the Buddha - he also pointed out that without a full understanding of worldly happiness one's wisdom is necessarily incomplete.

There **is** happiness in the world - the trouble is, it never lasts. People try to find happiness through status, health, beauty, family, possessions, and of course they succeed - up to a point. But none of these things can ever provide **permanent** happiness and that, ultimately, is the only thing that will ever really satisfy us.

Being made redundant is *dukkha* - so is getting a pay-rise. Getting cancer is *dukkha* - so is being young and healthy. Being criticised for being inconsiderate is *dukkha* - so is being considerate. Feeling that the world doesn't understand you is *dukkha* - so is thinking you have all the answers. And wanting to be free from *dukkha* is also *dukkha*.

The Buddha said that all things - all aspects of experience - are essentially unsatisfactory, they are all *dukkha*.

In the final analysis, every aspect of experience is suffering or *dukkha* because every aspect of experience is transient. Yet, the Buddha said, complete permanent happiness **can** be found - but not where we normally look.

The Four Noble Truths:
The Origin of Suffering

The first truth stated, 'There is suffering' - the second states that suffering has an origin, a cause.

Like all the noble truths, this statement is so simple that it might be easy to underestimate its crucial significance.

Many people believe that suffering occurs in our lives quite fortuitously; that pain and distress afflict us unpredictably and at random. For anyone who holds such a view, the problem of suffering can never be solved; there is no way out.

The Buddha stated that there is a cause of *dukkha*. Distress, unhappiness, anguish, despair - these things are not accidental and, critically, they are not inescapable.

So what is the cause of suffering?

Some people attribute their unhappiness to a lack of the resources necessary to buy their way to paradise. They believe that, if only they had a sufficiently high material standard of living, their problems would drop away. Others make the assumption that the root-cause of suffering is political or social injustice, or the degradation of the environment. Others still are convinced that their unhappiness is due to psychological causes - some childhood trauma, perhaps, has left them emotionally scarred.

The Buddha dismissed all such theories. He discovered through his own experience that suffering is always caused by craving.

When the Buddha spoke of craving, he was using the term in a subtler, more far-reaching way than our customary usage of the word allows. Essentially, craving means wanting things to be different from the way they are. This, the Buddha said, is the origin of all the suffering in the world.

If a man doesn't have much money and he wants a lot of money, then he suffers. If a woman is outraged by government corruption, believing such things should not happen, then she suffers. If people become incensed about cruelties inflicted on them in childhood, feeling that somehow it **should** have been different, then they suffer.

Craving is rooted in ignorance - an ignoring of the true nature of reality, an ignoring of the way things actually are.

The hallmark of craving is psychological dependence. Whenever we crave, we are emotionally attached to a particular end-result. Whenever we crave, we are - subtly or not so subtly - dependent on getting something. Or we are dependent on getting rid of something. Or we are dependent on becoming something different - a better parent maybe, better educated, more attractive, richer, thinner. Only when our actions are free from any form of dependency are they free from craving and do not cause suffering.

People can crave for food, money, sex; they can crave for world peace or for the elimination of poverty; they can crave for enlightenment. The Buddha said that craving leads to suffering - however altruistic or exalted the object craved for.

It is crucial to recognise that the problem lies with our own responses - not with whatever it is we want or don't want. No object, no thing, has the power to make us crave, no matter how attractive we might find it. Craving is always something we choose to do, even though we might not be clearly conscious that that is the case.

Being unable to afford to go on holiday, never being appreciated by the boss, having uncommunicative or badly-behaved children, illness, separation, death - none of these things need make us suffer. We only suffer when we resist. We only suffer when we are attached to things being a certain way - when we feel that we **should** be appreciated, we **should** remain healthy, we shouldn't die.

The Four Noble Truths:
The Cessation of Suffering

After the truth about the origin of suffering, there follows the truth about its cessation.

The third truth makes the definitive statement that suffering can end - completely and permanently. Every trace of unhappiness and distress can utterly disappear. As craving - wanting things to be different - is the cause of suffering, so the end of craving is the end of suffering.

The ending of suffering is *nibbana* (or *nirvana*), enlightenment. This is the goal of the Buddha's path - the goal, in fact, of all effective spiritual paths.

Descriptions of enlightenment are notoriously prone to misinterpretation. The Buddha usually described enlightenment in negative terms, in terms of what is missing rather than what is present. *Nibbana*, he said, is the cessation of ignorance, craving and hatred; *nibbana* is the cessation of suffering. Such negative terms are, in general, less likely to be misunderstood.

Nevertheless, wrong ideas about enlightenment are commonplace, even in Buddhist circles. One group of wrong ideas centres around the misunderstanding that all human behaviour is based in craving; and so, if we get rid of craving, we can no longer eat, work, relate to others – do anything in fact at all. In Buddhist philosophy this is known as the annihilationist view of enlightenment.

Enlightenment is the cessation of suffering, not the cessation of action. The Buddha himself, after he became enlightened, spent forty-five years teaching thousands of people the way to *nibbana*.

Enlightenment is the cessation of craving, not the cessation of preference. The Buddha preferred to teach; other enlightened people may prefer not to teach. If someone before enlightenment has a particular interest in teaching or people or food or anything else, there is no reason why that interest should not continue after he or she has completed the path.

Another major group of wrong ideas about enlightenment centres around what is called the eternalist view. This essentially sees *nibbana* as the acquisition of all good things, for ever. It sees *nibbana* as a permanent heavenly existence of bliss, power, omniscience, security.

But enlightenment is not unlimited pleasure. It is more accurate to say that it is freedom from attachment to good things or bad, freedom from attachment to pleasure or pain.

Note that pain and suffering are not synonymous. If someone who has attained enlightenment breaks his or her arm, it will still hurt; if he or she is insulted or abused, there may still be mental pain. The crucial difference is that the enlightened person totally accepts his circumstances. He knows that pain is a fact of life, just like pleasure. Neither lasts, neither is a problem, neither needs to be resisted or clung to.

Enlightenment is not learning to cope with distress nor is it merely a reduction in the unsatisfactoriness in our lives. It is the ending of **all** suffering, a total revolution.

Hearing this, many have effectively mythologised *nibbana* to the point where they believe that it is actually no longer attainable. But given sufficient determination, correct instruction and proper application, it is still possible for anyone to realise the goal of the Buddha's path.

The Four Noble Truths:
The Path

The problem - suffering - has been identified, its origin defined and the fact that it can be overcome established. The fourth truth states that there is a path to the ending of suffering.

Practically all of the Buddha's teachings are an exposition of this path to enlightenment. Many spiritual teachers have spoken about enlightenment - it was the particular genius of the Buddha that he laid down a precise and detailed course of training which has proved effective in different ages and different cultures and which remains both available and effective to this day.

The Buddha's path is often called the middle way because its essence is the avoidance of extremes. To indulge in extremes is actually easy. To devote oneself to satisfying one's physical appetites, for example, is easy; to indulge in the machismo of self-denial is also easy (it may take will-power but it needs little in the way of thought or sensitivity). The middle way is dynamic - it is not something that can be followed blindly or ritualistically.

The path is usually defined in terms of eight factors, eight aspects of physical, verbal and mental behaviour which need to be cultivated by those intent on coming to enlightenment. These are: speech, action, livelihood, mindfulness, effort, concentration, view and aim.

The eight factors can be grouped into three main divisions – ethics (comprising speech, action and livelihood); meditation (mindfulness, effort and concentration); and wisdom or understanding (view and aim).

The ethical division of the path is concerned with the restraint of selfish behaviour; the development of these factors requires a lifestyle that is considerate of others and as harmless as possible. Where ethics deals with physical and verbal action, meditation is concerned with the mind, learning to control and balance it so that it becomes an effective tool for the development of wisdom. In developing wisdom we come to know through our own experience what actually causes suffering and how to be free of it.

In broad terms, developing the appropriate level of ethical behaviour allows us to meditate correctly, which in turn brings about the arising of wisdom.

This does not mean that the three sections of the path are developed serially – in practical terms ethics, meditation and understanding are dynamically interdependent and the person following the path correctly is working on all three groups together.

At one stage in his practice, for example, a meditator may recognise that he needs to pay more attention to the content of his speech and restrain a tendency to be economical with the truth. In attempting to do this, he grows in wisdom – he gets a clearer picture of precisely what honesty is, as well as gaining an experiential understanding of why honesty is a positive quality. Thanks to this greater clarity of vision, he finds it all the easier to control his speech.

Because they are interdependent, none of the sections of the path can be omitted. To minimise the importance of ethical conduct, for example, as some have tried to do, renders the path ineffective. Someone who acts in an habitually selfish manner will find that he is so caught up in his own concerns that he is incapable of seeing beyond those very limited horizons.

The Buddha described this path to *nibbana* as 'beautiful in the beginning, beautiful in the middle, beautiful in the end'. Anyone who sincerely applies him- or herself to the path will find that suffering diminishes, right from the very start. The greater the application, the greater the reduction in suffering.

In fact, getting rid of things is the keynote of the path – getting rid of craving, getting rid of all the things we do which make us suffer. We gain no credentials, no status, from following the path; we acquire nothing that the world would value. Simply, we do away with suffering.

A Teacher

Even though the four truths are clearly expressed, even though the path is described in detail, following the path is not always easy. What constitutes a middle way is different for each one of us. How we should best apply ourselves to the path is a very individual matter.

We each have a unique set of strengths and weaknesses; we each have our own particular blind-spots. Books can help but they can take us only so far. To make real progress, we need a guide. We ourselves are in a sense too close to the problem - a teacher has the perspective and the detachment necessary to steer us in the right direction.

Spiritual teachers, of course, vary in quality. Some have a sound intellectual understanding of the path but little practical experience of it. Others may have plenty of experience but lack the communication skills necessary to convey what they know to other people. The ideal teacher is one who has himself travelled the path from beginning to end and who can inspire his students and guide them towards the same goal.

Should we find a skilled teacher, we maximise this good fortune by following his or her instructions to the best of our ability. As one who illuminates the path to the ending of suffering, he or she is the most valuable person we will ever encounter.

It is essential that we have a guide but, in the final analysis, it is we who must walk the path.

A man once asked the Buddha, 'If you know enlightenment and the path to enlightenment, why is it that some of your students get there and others don't?'

The Buddha replied, 'Well, you know the town of Rajagaha, you know how to get to it from here. Can you be certain that everyone you direct there will arrive?'

Similarly, the Buddha pointed out, he knew enlightenment and he knew the path that leads to it but he could not be held accountable for how people chose to apply themselves to his instructions. 'I am simply the one,' he said, 'who shows the way.'

Rebirth & The Law of Kamma

Some of the ideas within Buddhism are undoubtedly alien to mainstream modern western views. A notable example of this is rebirth. Some western Buddhist writers have chosen to gloss over this subject, perhaps feeling that it might alienate their readers and so be counterproductive.

The concept of rebirth is central to what the Buddha said about beings and their behaviour. Without an understanding of rebirth, much of the teaching will not make sense.

Buddhism, in common with other oriental philosophies, states that we have more than one life, that we have lived many times before and that we will be reborn after death again and again.

The belief in reincarnation or rebirth has existed in some form throughout recorded history. Even in the most materialistic cultures, there have been instances of individuals who have claimed to remember previous existences. Some of these cases have been thoroughly investigated and, although the evidence can only ever be circumstantial, the correlation between the memories of the individuals and established historical facts cannot adequately be explained in any other way.

According to Buddhist cosmology, in addition to this human realm, there are thirty different realms of existence into which beings can be reborn. Life in the higher realms is predominantly pleasant. In the lower realms it is predominantly painful. In the human realm there is roughly an equal balance of pleasure and pain.

What determines the kind of life we are born into?

If we act selfishly, we experience painful results - in a human birth or even in a lower realm; if we act unselfishly, we experience pleasurable results - in a human birth or in a higher realm. This is the essence of the law of *kamma* (or *karma*). The quality of our life is determined by the actions we make.

Though the basic principle of the law of *kamma* is straightforward, the details of its operation can be extraordinarily complex; all of us have lived many, many lives before and performed countless actions, both good and bad. While some broad guidelines can be laid down - stealing, for example, is said traditionally to result in future poverty - we cannot predict for certain exactly when a particular action will come to fruition, nor precisely how its result will manifest. What we can know is that, when present conditions are suitable, past actions **will** have results.

The law of *kamma* has nothing to do with punishment or reward. Like the law of gravity, it is a natural law of life that operates automatically. If we kill or steal, we may or may not dodge the legal system but at some point down the line - whether in this lifetime now or in a life to come - we will experience painful results. If we are generous and considerate, a favourable outcome in the future is certain.

Buddhism states that we will die and be reborn time and time again. Dependent on our actions, some of our lives will be predominantly happy and successful, some will be restricted and oppressive. But whether heaven-states, hell-states or anything in between - none of them ever lasts. This endless round of birth and death is known as *samsara* - literally, 'perpetual wandering'. Because nothing ever lasts, true happiness can never be found within *samsara*. *Samsara* is *dukkha*, it is inherently unsatisfactory.

The Buddha's path leads to the cessation of *dukkha* - to the escape from *samsara*.

Kamma & The Path

Enlightenment is not the result of unselfish actions. No matter how generous you are with your material possessions, no matter how much of your time and energy you sacrifice for the good of others, these things alone cannot lead to the final destruction of suffering. They will result in future happiness – even in a prolonged heavenly existence – but, as we have seen, such states cannot last.

Enlightenment is beyond unselfishness and selfishness. It is beyond action and result. The path, however, is all about action. It deals with the development of particular actions (*kamma*) specifically geared towards producing a mind sufficiently subtle and intelligent to come to see things as they are.

For those intent on enlightenment, a principle of crucial importance is self-responsibility. In many ways, the starting-point of the whole path comes when we begin to understand that happiness and unhappiness are the results not of external conditions but rather of our own internal responses and our own actions.

Quite a few people, for example, believe that if only they had more money – perhaps just another couple of thousand a year – they would be happy. They wouldn't have to worry about winter electricity bills or unexpected car repairs; they could buy the clothes they wanted, go on holidays, go out for meals and not have to concern themselves with budgeting and saving. If they had enough money, everything would be all right.

When such people start to observe their experience more carefully, it becomes obvious that there is no direct link between the quality of their mental state and their current financial status. What **does** condition their mental state is the way they choose to respond to their relative wealth or lack of it - whether they accept that they can't afford a new jacket or whether they resent the fact.

We are responsible for our own actions, physical, verbal and mental - actions have results (whether we believe they do or not). We chose in the past to perform selfish and unselfish actions; the results of those actions have brought about our present circumstances. Hence we have effectively chosen whatever situation we find ourselves in, whether it is to our liking or not. In the moment, now, we choose to act selfishly or we choose to act unselfishly. With every selfish or unselfish action we make, we are shaping our own future. We are responsible for our lives - past, present and future.

The more clearly we come to see this, the less able are we to believe that life is 'not fair'. We can no longer feel so justified in blaming everyone and everything for our own perceived misfortunes; we can no longer feel so frustrated or impotent.

In accepting responsibility for our actions, we acquire power - the power to transform the way we act now. And how we act **now** is what matters.

For anyone who wishes to take up the Buddha's path, the past is totally irrelevant. It does not matter in the least what we've done (or what we believe we've done) in the past. What we've had done to us (or what we believe we've had done to us) is equally unimportant.

However cruel or destructive we may have been, however painful our present circumstances, the path starts from here and now. And if we find life at the moment to be enjoyable and rewarding, such results of past unselfishness need provide no occasion for complacency. What actually counts is how we respond to those results now. We can respond skilfully - or unselfishly - to painful conditions; we can restrain our annoyance, for example, at the moodiness of a partner. We can respond unskilfully - or selfishly - to positive conditions; getting conceited, perhaps, at our own successes.

Walking the path, we learn to discriminate experientially between these two basic types of response. The ability to choose skilful actions and to restrain unskilful ones creates a mind which is calmer, more confident, balanced.

Though *dukkha* can never be eradicated by unselfishness alone, the restraint of unskilful actions and the cultivation of skilful ones is fundamental to success on the path.

The Precepts

The Buddha formulated five precepts which define the level of ethical conduct necessary for success in the training. The five cover those areas of behaviour where restraint is essential if the practice is going to make a real difference to one's life. Without such restraint, one cannot develop the subtlety of mind necessary for meditation.

The traditional wording of the first precept is, 'I undertake the rule of training to refrain from killing or harming living creatures.'

The enlightened person is quintessentially harmless. Deliberately destroying life or inflicting pain is completely incongruous with a desire for enlightenment. The person who undertakes the precepts does his best always to avoid harming beings. He or she will not hunt or fish; he will avoid killing spiders, ants, slugs, wasps.

Of course, some killing is an inevitable part of life. Every time we wash – every time we breathe – countless micro-organisms are destroyed. Every time we walk across a lawn we cannot help but kill living creatures.

When we wash or walk across a lawn, or when we accidentally step on a snail, we are not breaking the first precept. If accidentally we cause injury or even death to another human being – in a car crash, for example – we are not breaking the first precept. The precepts only deal with deliberately harmful action.

The second precept states, 'I undertake the rule of training to refrain from taking that which is not given.'

Someone committed to the path not only resists any temptation to steal but, further, he or she will be scrupulous about, for example, returning borrowed property or restraining the urge to read other people's mail. He does his best not to take liberties.

The third precept is concerned with sexual conduct. Any sexual practice which causes harm – whether to oneself or to others – is to be avoided. An adulterous relationship, for example, not only triggers guilt and apprehension in the individuals concerned – it is also likely to cause extreme distress to other people.

In keeping the precepts, we benefit not only ourselves but also all those with whom we come into contact. Refusing to add to the negativity in the world is an extremely positive action.

In undertaking the fourth precept, a meditator restrains the urge to indulge in all forms of harmful speech, the traditional classification comprising lying, harsh speech, slander and gossip.

For most people, although some minor adjustments may be necessary, keeping the first three precepts poses no particular difficulty. Right speech, however, can be more problematic. It is often very tempting, for example, to twist the truth in order to present a desired impression. Nor is it always easy to avoid being drawn into a conversation about an absent party which degenerates into little more than character assassination.

Speech **is** a difficult area - it is important to note that the wording of the precepts describes them as 'rules of training to refrain from'. This acknowledges the fact that keeping the precepts is not always an easy thing to do. Unless, however, we make the attempt to avoid harmful speech, we will find that the mind is often ill-at-ease and is frequently beset with recrimination.

The final precept states, 'I undertake the rule of training to refrain from all forms of intoxicants and mind-altering substances.'

The immediate purpose of the precepts is to render the mind capable of meditation. Intentionally to indulge in alcohol or psychotropic drugs is incompatible with the attempt to meditate. To walk the path successfully means to attain an increasingly accurate vision of reality - therefore, any form of escapism is counterproductive.

The precepts are a means to an end. They are not absolute moral injunctions - rather are they practical guidelines for controlling forms of behaviour inimical to the path to enlightenment.

The precepts form the foundation for the whole of the path. Without them, progress is not possible. Unethical conduct is invariably selfish. Such selfishness is completely inconsistent with a path which aims at destroying all selfishness.

The Practice of Meditation

Most statues of the Buddha show him seated in meditation. Meditation is the heart of the Buddhist way.

There are countless different forms of meditation – the central practice of the Buddha's path to enlightenment is known as *vipassana* or insight meditation. While most other meditation practices are primarily concerned with control, the essence of *vipassana* is observation. Practising *vipassana*, the meditator endeavours to pay attention to the rise and fall of whatever aspect of physical or mental experience is most prominent in the moment.

Many people have the idea that meditation is something unworldly and obscure. *Vipassana* meditation is straightforward and pragmatic. It does not aim at producing altered states of consciousness or psychic phenomena – it simply involves the unbiased observation of whatever is present.

For the practice of *vipassana*, the meditator needs a room where he or she will be undisturbed for the duration of the session - ideally, a daily minimum of half-an-hour. Meditating at the same time every day can assist in establishing the practice as a regular habit.

It is not necessary to sit in the lotus position or even cross-legged. For most westerners such postures are difficult or even impossible without years of practice. To sit on a straight-backed chair is perfectly acceptable. What counts is that one's posture should be sustainable for the half-hour or longer - the body upright but not strained, alert yet relaxed. The eyes should be closed, the hands cupped loosely together in the lap.

The attention is then gently directed towards the sensation in the abdomen that comes about dependent on the breathing. The rise and fall of this sensation forms the main focus of the practice. After each rise and fall, the meditator silently counts - 'one' after the first breath, 'two' after the second and so on, up until 'ten', after which he starts again at 'one'.

The breath should be natural - not in any way forced or manipulated. One's relationship to the breath should mirror the way in which one relates to all other aspects of experience encountered in meditation.

What the new meditator soon discovers is that paying attention to one object is not easy. The mind wanders. He may get as far as 'four' and then find himself in the middle of a row with his ex-wife. Whenever he loses the thread of the meditation in such a way, he needs to acknowledge what has happened and gently return the mind to the observation of the rise and fall of the abdomen and start counting again at 'one'.

The rise and fall sensation serves as an anchor for the practice, in the sense that it provides a focal point to which the mind can be repeatedly returned. Good meditation practice is inclusive - the sounds, thoughts, memories of which we become aware while attending to the sensation in the abdomen should not be regarded as distractions.

Rather are they themselves equally valid objects of meditation, which we can observe to rise and fall.

Not excluding other objects in the practice means that we acknowledge whatever interrupts our attempts to pay attention to the rise and fall and the counting. These interruptions can simply be labelled. For example, we might identify a sound as 'traffic' or just as 'hearing'. Thoughts about a row, remembered or hypothetical, can be labelled as 'memory' or 'thinking'. Many believe that in order to meditate one has to get rid of thinking. As far as the *vipassana* practice is concerned, thinking is just another aspect of experience, no more or less important than anything else.

If any physical discomfort should arise during the practice – perhaps a bit of tension, the odd pain or itch – it just needs to be noted (as 'pain' or 'itch') and the attention returned to the rise and fall sensation. Any urge to shift about or scratch should similarly be noted; it does not need to be acted on. To move would be to resort to control and manipulation; in meditation all we need to do is observe.

Ignorance & The 3 Marks

The object of *vipassana* meditation is to learn to observe all our experience in a dispassionate and systematic way, free of prejudice and preconception. The reason for this is simple. Buddhism states that suffering only arises when we see things wrongly. This flawed way of seeing is what the Buddha termed ignorance. He went on to say that such ignorance is chosen. In pursuit of our dreams of happiness, we choose - albeit usually unconsciously - to disregard some crucial facts of experience.

Vipassana meditation reverses this process of ignorance.

So what do we ignore that causes us to suffer? The Buddha identified three attributes common to all aspects of experience - the 'three marks'. He said that all physical and mental phenomena are transient (*anicca*), inherently unsatisfactory (*dukkha*) and that they are *anatta* - literally 'non-self': they have no unchanging core and, ultimately, cannot be owned or controlled. Transience, unsatisfactoriness and *anatta* are the facts that we ignore.

On one level, people do recognise that things are transient. We all know that fashions change, seasons come and go. We are happy to accept that civilisations decay, mountains erode and that whole planets come into existence and are eventually destroyed. We accept, perhaps grudgingly, that friendships end and that people grow old and die.

Whatever we think we know intellectually, our resistance to transience runs deep. A mother, for example, may refuse to acknowledge that her children are now adult and that parental guidance is no longer appropriate. She suffers because she will not accept the fact that her role is now completely different. A close friend chooses to go and live halfway across the world; this could only make us suffer if we had assumed that the friendship would last. To assume that anything will last is to ignore transience.

We also refuse to see that the objects we crave for are not capable of providing the lasting satisfaction we demand from them – we ignore their unsatisfactoriness. A man or woman desperate to maintain a relationship, for example, will cling to an idealised image of their partner, refusing to admit to the growing evidence of incompatibility.

Many people spend much of their lives in the fruitless pursuit of some form of perfection – the perfect partner, the perfect car, the perfect sound-system, the perfect holiday ... The dreams of tropical sunshine, freedom from the daily grind and exotic food are invariably dashed by the reality of oppressive heat, long waits in queues and digestive problems.

The third attribute of experience which we ignore is that we cannot actually control things as we would wish. For example, we cannot prevent our bodies from malfunctioning or our skin from eventually wrinkling. Nor can we exercise complete control over, say, our creative talents. A writer may have some days when he seems to be full of interesting new ideas; on others, he can't think in anything other than clichés. Bodies and minds are *anatta* – ultimately, they are not answerable to our personal will.

Because ignorance of transience, unsatisfactoriness and *anatta* is so ingrained, the reversal of ignorance is quite an undertaking. Because it **is** difficult, we have to give ourselves the best possible conditions for training ourselves to see things as they really are.

Firstly, while observation of any of the marks erodes ignorance, in practical terms transience is the mark which is usually emphasised because it is generally the easiest to perceive.

Secondly, through the practice of formal seated meditation, we give ourselves the opportunity to cultivate our powers of observation in the most conducive of circumstances, free from external distractions.

Half-an-hour a day, however, is not enough. The seated practice has to be supported by the attempt to bring awareness of transience into all aspects of our lives.

Mindfulness

The fundamental skill necessary for successful *vipassana* practice is mindfulness. Mindfulness is in fact nothing unusual – it is something that all of us employ every day.

Mindfulness in the general sense is simply an awareness of present experience. If we are consciously aware of what is going on rather than lost in fantasy, we are mindful. In the context of the Buddha's path, however, mindfulness has an extra dimension.

A meditator who is mindful is not only aware of what is going on but, crucially, he or she is seeking to focus on the transient nature of all aspects of the experience. This is part of what is known technically as 'clear comprehension'. It does not matter how mindful someone might be – if he is not aware of transience, insight will not arise. Someone trying to sort out a malfunctioning computer programme may be exquisitely mindful but, without awareness of the three marks, he is not going to gain any meditative understanding.

The level of detail one might perceive will vary dependent on prevailing conditions. Where there are a lot of distractions – jostling for standing-room on an overcrowded commuter train, for example - mindfulness will tend to be more general than it might be while sitting quietly in a chair.

On the train there is a whole stream of objects that seem to demand our attention. No matter how chaotic it is, all the objects are transient and all are valid objects of meditation. We are not, however, going to be able to isolate and pay attention to individual sensations to the degree that we can while we're sitting relaxing.

It is particularly important to remember exactly why it is that we are learning to develop mindfulness anyway - that, in the last analysis, our purpose is the total eradication of suffering.

If we are to attain enlightenment, formal meditation needs to be part of a regime that aims at cultivating mindfulness in every aspect of daily life. Mindfulness has to be developed on a systematic basis. Wherever we are not mindful, there we continue to ignore. It is in those unexamined areas that assumptions of permanence and satisfactoriness go unchallenged, subverting our attempts to find true happiness.

To assist the development of systematic mindfulness, a scheme for classifying experience is invaluable.

Our usual western classification divides experience into the objective and the subjective - the external world and the internal world. The Buddhist template is quite different. Its basic dichotomy is body and mind.

Body does not refer just to one's own physical body - it includes **all** materiality. In the Buddhist scheme of analysis, tables, rivers, computers, plants, other people's bodies are all classified as 'body'.

Everything that is not body is mind - emotions, ideas, thoughts, memories, ideals, awareness itself.

While this is the most basic division of experience, body and mind themselves can be analysed into far more intricate detail. Buddhism is full of lists which subdivide experience in different ways. However simple or complex, their purpose is always the same: to provide a template for the development of mindfulness.

The aspect of experience most readily apprehended is body, notably one's own body. (This is why in formal seated meditation a physical sensation is selected as the major focus of the practice.) Whatever activity one is engaged in, it is always possible to direct the attention towards the body.

This is another aspect of clear comprehension – knowing which objects to attend to. Essentially, we have to pay attention to that which is most prominent. We pay attention not to our ideas about things – rather we attend to the raw sense-data itself. Whenever we lose mindfulness, the most effective course of action is simply to return the attention to physical sensations. When in doubt, keep it simple.

Walking down the street, a meditator attends to the rise and fall of physical sensations as the arms swing or the feet touch the ground. Sitting down for a cup of coffee, he is mindful of the sensation of pressure where his thigh contacts the edge of the chair, of the heat of the coffee as he drinks.

Even in an activity which is predominantly mental, such as working at a computer or reading a book, there is always a physical component – the fingers moving over the keyboard or the hand reaching out to turn a page.

If the daily half-hour of seated practice is supplemented by the attempt to attend to bodily activity throughout the day, the potential opportunities for paying attention to the rise and fall of things are greatly increased.

With repeated application over the days and months, the meditator's ability to observe transience strengthens. Every time he notes that a posture has changed - from sitting to standing, from standing to walking, from walking to lying down - or that a physical sensation has arisen and then disappeared, his belief that things can be permanent is weakened.

The Meditative Lifestyle

Meditation is a skill like any other - the more time we devote to the practice, the more proficient we become. The more proficient we become, the more in touch we are with ourselves and the world.

While most of us find that our initial attempts at cultivating awareness of body can seem self-conscious and to a degree artificial, with persistence we can establish the habit of paying mindful attention in an increasingly natural way. It is not a question of changing the way we walk or sit or stand but rather of bringing awareness to the things we do. Insight meditation, as we have said, is not concerned with control or manipulation but simply with observing the transience of whatever is there.

There may well, however, be certain activities we habitually engage in which we will find less than helpful if we want to develop mindfulness.

Undertaking the precepts immediately removes many of the major obstacles to successful practice. By resolving not to harm others (whether physically or verbally) and by respecting their property and their established relationships, we both reduce the areas of potential conflict in our lives and also minimise the occurrence of such mental states as guilt, apprehension and remorse. The decision not to drink alcohol or take psychotropic drugs further supports the development of clear awareness.

How we choose to make a living is in this context an important issue, occupying as it does a substantial portion of our time and attention. Traditionally, trading in arms, intoxicants and poisons, and selling animals for slaughter are listed as modes of livelihood deleterious to the attempt to meditate. Basically, any job or profession which is liable to cause harm to other beings should be avoided if our minds are to be sufficiently settled for the practice of mindfulness.

In addition to ethical questions, we may also need to consider the volume of activities we engage in. Both inveterate socialisers and workaholics will find meditation very difficult. Their minds will be so cluttered with people and parties on the one hand and deadlines and assignments on the other that they will be far too agitated to pay attention to the present moment.

Such meditators, if they are serious about the practice, will find the lack of mental quietude so frustrating that they will want to make adjustments to their lifestyles. A meditator may resolve, for example, only to go out at weekends, to shelve his evening classes in computer graphics or martial arts, or to stop bringing work home from the office.

Responsibilities and relationships, however, do not themselves preclude meditative progress. While the lifestyle of a Buddhist monk or nun is specifically designed to provide circumstances which are as ideal as is possible, it is still entirely possible for a lay person – with a family and career – to become enlightened.

The Correct Use of Energy

Most of us in the West have been conditioned to believe that success in any field is dependent on hard work; the greater the effort, the higher the return. Operating on the basis of this view, people get to the top in business, sport, politics, the media. For so many, this mode of behaviour represents the line of least resistance which they automatically adopt in any new venture.

Unfortunately, when it comes to meditation, this approach does not work. Learning what constitutes an appropriate level of energy in meditation is undoubtedly one of the most difficult areas of the practice.

The majority of meditators try too hard. They use far too much force in directing the mind towards the sensation of rise and fall in the abdomen and often in their attempts to establish mindfulness in daily life. As a result, they experience a lot of physical and mental tension. Not only is the meditation uncomfortable, it is also unproductive – with this background of tension, the mind is agitated and unintelligent.

One of the reasons why the correct level of meditative energy is not easy to establish is that it does not feel effortful enough. Given a spectrum of effort ranging from teeth-gritted maximum at one extreme to a lazy zero at the other, the correct degree of energy for meditation – from our subjective point of view – can seem dangerously close to inactivity.

For successful meditation we need a light touch. Turning the mind towards the meditation object does not require any physical effort. Interestingly, many of us are unaware that we use physical energy when undertaking mental work. Many meditators can be seen to be straining physically – frowning, clenching the jaw, shoulders raised in tension, hands clasped tightly together. If there is any physical tension or discomfort, it is more than likely that we are trying too hard.

The urge to try too hard is always volitional but, because over-effort can be so habitual, it is far from easy to detect. Once we have discovered for ourselves that over-effort just does not work, we can by means of mindfulness set about restraining it. We cannot succeed in overcoming it unless we are fully aware of our desire to force the pace. Continuing to develop mindfulness, both in and out of the formal seated practice, we come to see exactly how it is we choose to apply effort in the moment.

Turning the mind to the object of meditation requires a minimum of effort. Look at the first word on this page; now look at the last. The level of energy you used to read those words was akin to the level appropriate in meditation. It seems in a way too simple – a long way from the strain and tension which the forceful westerner associates with something serious like meditation.

Right meditative effort is sustainable. Having established an appropriate level of energy, it becomes possible to direct the mind to the momentary birth and death of phenomena again and again and again. The key to the correct use of energy is gentle repetition – not force. It is the repeated observation of transience that leads to the eradication of suffering.

A Sense of Urgency

The Buddha's last words were, 'All conditioned things are impermanent. Strive on with diligence.' During his lifetime, he frequently advised his followers to make the most of their opportunity to practise the teaching. 'Meditate,' he told them. 'Do not be slothful; be not remorseful later.'

It seems paradoxical – how do we balance such an instruction with the light, practically effortless touch necessary in meditation? While over-effort in the seated practice is fruitless, commitment to the path is essential.

Commitment is action. Commitment to the Buddha's path means **doing** the practice – meditating every day and attempting repeatedly to be systematically mindful.

There are those who consider themselves to be committed and yet their practice is sporadic. Many such people believe – quite sincerely – that tomorrow, or next week, or when their life is less hectic, they're **really** going to start applying themselves. It is easy to think that our time is limitless. It's not.

The Buddha once said to Pasenadi, King of Kosala: 'Suppose a reliable informant comes to your court from the east and reports that a vast mountain, as tall as the sky, is moving towards Kosala, crushing all living creatures in its wake. Suppose you get similar reports about mountains moving, from the west and the north and the south. Hemmed in on all sides, what would you do?'

'What could I do,' Pasenadi replied, 'but practise the Dhamma?'

The mountains might not actually be moving, the Buddha continued, but for all living creatures old age and death advance inexorably ...

None of us knows how much longer we have to live. At any moment death can interrupt our plans. Further, teachers of the path are also mortal. And the Buddha's teaching itself – like everything else – will at some point cease to exist.

Given the essential vulnerability of our situation, if we have had the good fortune to come across an effective way to truth, it makes every sense to take advantage of our opportunity.

If we are going to become enlightened, we need commitment, persistence, a certain single-mindedness of approach. We also need to meditate. But if our meditation is to be effective, it is essential that we learn to put to one side the drive and ambition which obstruct mindful attention.

Concentration

When it comes to describing mind and its functioning, the West in general does not have a tradition of precise definition. Terms such as consciousness and perception – even mind itself – are used to cover a whole range of meanings. Concentration is no exception.

In contrast, the precise and comprehensive nature of the Buddhist terminology of mind is striking. In one English translation of a Buddhist text, for example, sixteen different words had to be rendered by the single English term 'desire'.

In Buddhism, concentration is specifically one-pointedness – the narrowing of the focus of the mind. Every time we choose to pay attention to the breath – indeed, every time we select any object at all to attend to – we are concentrating the mind.

Like mindfulness, concentration is something all of us employ. Crossing a road, driving a car, holding a conversation – all these activities demand a certain degree of concentration. The level of concentration, however, can vary enormously. Someone engrossed in a novel is concentrating; a goalkeeper facing a penalty kick is concentrating; a hermit meditating in a Himalayan cave is also concentrating.

Of the many different types of meditation, the majority are methods of developing deeper and deeper levels of concentration. The specific object of meditation can range from a mental visualisation to a candle-flame to a mantra. Repeatedly focusing on such an object, the meditator can experience states of increasing calm and tranquillity.

The reason such practices are so popular and ubiquitous is that they are very pleasurable. As the mind concentrates, it gradually withdraws from the external world. The body becomes very relaxed and comfortable; the mind loses interest in worries and concerns. It seems like a real holiday from the stresses of everyday existence. In deep concentration, the mind completely withdraws from the material universe and experiences states of great bliss.

As far as the path to enlightenment is concerned, however, such states have limited value. No matter how pleasurable, no matter how meaningful they might seem, concentrated states in themselves do nothing to increase our understanding of suffering and its cause. And yet the ability to concentrate is an essential requirement for the *vipassana* meditator.

Without concentration, mindfulness remains too superficial. Without concentration, the mind is filled with numerous objects all jostling for our attention. The calmness and poise of the concentrated mind provides the perfect support for the development of mindfulness.

The level of concentration necessary for *vipassana* meditation is that at which the mind is settled and alert and able to watch sensory data arising and passing away. The problem with deeper levels of concentration is that the mind is so withdrawn that sounds, sensations, thoughts are no longer experienced.

The level appropriate to *vipassana* is not something that only a gifted few can achieve. While some initially find concentration elusive, with repeated application – with mindfulness and the correct use of energy – it is a skill that anyone can develop.

Putting It Into Practice

What type of experience might the new meditator encounter?

Each of us comes to the practice from a different background – some people already have some knowledge of Buddhism; others are completely new to it all. We all have different skills, different expectations. Some feel quite at home with the practice; others may find their initial experiences a little daunting.

It is not unknown for a meditator to sit down for his first session, to apply the mind to the sensation in the abdomen as instructed and to find that his attention settles effortlessly on the rise and fall and the counting. He remains attentive yet relaxed and the half-hour seems to pass rapidly.

The next day, he sits down to meditate again, fired with enthusiasm. After five minutes, he is tense and irritable; the mind feels heavy and unwieldy and, despite all his efforts to the contrary, he keeps dipping in and out of unconsciousness.

There is a wide range of experience that can occur in meditation. Some days the practice may seem plagued by sleepiness; other days by agitation and seemingly constant thinking.

There will be times as well when the mind suddenly goes clear and still and the meditator becomes quite engrossed in the whole process of observation. Whether he is attending to the sensation in the abdomen, to sounds or the occasional thought, he is able to watch objects rising and falling with ease.

As concentration deepens, the meditator may experience unusual and often pleasurable physical phenomena. The hands or even the whole body can seem to swell up in size. The body may feel extremely light, as though about to rise up off the chair; or it may feel very heavy, as though set in concrete. Hairs may stand on end or itching sensations may occur, typically described as 'like ants crawling on the skin'. It is also not uncommon to see light in the mind. This may take the form of washes of colour or discs of light of various sizes.

Such experiences can seem quite intriguing, particularly when they are happening for the first time; it can be tempting to try to prolong them or make them recur. Their only value as far as the *vipassana* meditator is concerned, however, is that they can be noted as transient.

For the meditator who is applying too much effort in his practice, the predominant physical experience is one of discomfort. Pains may arise in the shoulders, the back or the legs; there may be facial tension or headaches. When the meditator learns to stop trying too hard, the pains will cease. Until that time, he should simply label these physical sensations and note that they are transient.

While we may initially be under the impression that such pains are continuous and long-lasting, precise observation will reveal that in fact they are momentary.

Aches, pains, itches – they arise and instantly die away. A similar pain may then arise close by, but it should be noted that it is actually a different pain, a new pain.

Subjective experience of time in meditation can vary enormously. When the mind is restless, the meditator is often all too aware of time and a half-hour session can seem to last at least twice as long. Many in such circumstances have been tempted to open their eyes and check the clock. Succumbing to such an urge will only exacerbate the tension and undermine the meditator's resolution to complete future sessions.

When concentration and interest are strong, on the other hand, there may be little or no awareness of time at all. At the end of the session, it can seem as though the time has flashed by.

Right mindfulness, as we have seen, is inclusive. One aspect of experience that new meditators frequently **exclude** is their own judgements about how their practice is developing. Thoughts like 'I'm never going to get this right!' – unless they are mindfully noted – will lead to all kinds of doubts and despondency. Thoughts along the lines of 'I've really got the hang of this now!' – unless mindfully noted – will lead to over-excitement and conceit.

However the practice goes, it is worth remembering that meditation is a skill to be learned. Acquiring the necessary expertise takes time and persistent application. Beware of assuming, however, that success in the practice is only possible off in the future, when mindfulness and concentration are perfectly developed. For the meditator who is applying himself correctly, insight can arise at any moment.

View

One discovery we make when we embark on the practice of meditation is that our beliefs and views – no matter how passionately held – are not present as some sort of continuous backdrop to our experience. They are in fact selected in the moment as chosen responses to particular circumstances.

A woman sits down to meditate. Unusually for her, her body soon becomes extremely relaxed; she feels as if her limbs have turned to liquid. She is intrigued by the calm and clarity and by the seeming effortlessness of the practice. Suddenly, a thought arises: 'This can't be right.' She picks up one of her habitual responses – a view which states that all the worthwhile things in life come from hard work. In seconds flat, the mental and physical ease evaporates as she forcefully re-applies herself to watching the rise and fall.

A view is a way of seeing. 'There is only one life', 'Capital punishment is never justified', 'Any film with sub-titles is boring', 'Nationalism is always divisive', 'British beef is best' – there is an infinite number of possible views. All of us have our own points of view, our own interpretations, our own unique ways of seeing things.

Views condition all aspects of our behaviour and have a profound effect on our lives. If someone truly believes that he only has this one lifetime, for example, he can have no fear that selfish behaviour will have any repercussions after death. Therefore, he has no reason not to try and get away with as much as he can.

While all views are chosen, we may not always be consciously aware of the choices we are making. Some people, for example, unconsciously assume that only oriental teachers really understand the Buddha's teaching. They therefore tend to accept the words of Thai or Tibetan teachers uncritically, while believing that western teachers know little more than they do themselves.

Another example of an unconscious view can be seen in the way that some western authors misconstrue certain aspects of the teaching, failing to realise that they are interpreting it through the filter of their own Judaeo-Christian conditioning. Their concept of enlightenment, for instance, may centre around moral perfection rather than transcendence.

Essentially, the views we choose to employ can be more or less consistent with the way things actually are.

Any action we perform which is based on an inaccurate view of reality will bring about increased suffering. Someone who insists on believing that everyone **should** be honest, for example, will experience distress whenever he comes across deliberate deception.

Any action based on an accurate view of reality, on the other hand, does not lead to suffering. Someone who understands that, ultimately, we all have to make our own mistakes and who tends not to interfere with other people's lives will not experience frustration if others reject his counsel.

In Buddhist terminology, inaccurate views are 'wrong' and accurate views 'right'. The meditative training enables us to examine our views as they arise. We gradually learn through experience and through study of the teaching which of our views promote suffering and which do not.

Perception

You're sitting in meditation and you hear a sound. You get annoyed. You think, 'Forgot to switch the phone off.' If mindfulness had been stronger, you could have noted the arising and ceasing of hearing and the subsequent arising of a label, 'phone ringing'.

In Buddhist terminology such a label is called a perception. Through perceptions we know what it is that we are experiencing. We hear, see, touch – it is only through the process of perception that we recognise **what** we hear, see and touch.

A perception can be fairly general – 'That's a painting' – or quite specific – 'That's a poor reproduction of Kandinsky's *Circle and Square*'. Perception is recognition – the process whereby we re-cognise the world – and we can only recognise what we have already encountered. If we know nothing of modern art, we could never label a picture as a Kandinsky, let alone evaluate it as an inferior reproduction.

Perceptions are not static. We can train our ability to discriminate in whatever field we choose. For example, someone might think that all Indian food is much the same. After six months' travelling round the subcontinent, he finds himself effortlessly differentiating between Assamese, Goan and Kashmiri cuisine.

Perception arises dependent on past actions. It arises automatically - the process of perception does not involve any thought or deliberation. In Buddhist terms, a perception is a resultant as opposed to an action (*kamma*). Resultants are the inevitable outcome of actions and do not themselves produce further effects.

Many people are deeply attached to perception. In fact, it could be said that intellectuality is nothing more than the pursuit and ordering of perceptions. It is not unknown for those who are intellectually inclined to try to think their way to enlightenment. But perceptions can only convey past knowledge and, no matter how elegantly the past is re-ordered, it can never lead to anything new. To approach enlightenment, we have to leave the past behind - enlightenment is the unknown.

Feelings & Responses

Imagine sifting through a box of old photographs. With each picture you experience a different feeling. Some of the images bring a warm, pleasurable tone to the mind. The feeling that arises as you look at others may be so intense that you immediately want to rip them up.

Feelings – like perceptions – are resultants; their arising cannot be controlled. Feelings are conditioned by past action. Positive unselfish actions give rise to pleasant feelings, selfish actions to painful feelings.

Another illustration: think of the most despicable thing you've ever done. The tone of the mind that accompanies that memory is a painful feeling – perhaps intensely painful. All feelings arise and pass away rapidly; no matter how strong they may be, they do not need to be acted upon.

In English, we use the terms 'feeling' and 'emotion' loosely and interchangeably. To the meditator, a feeling is purely the painful or pleasant tone of the mind (however strong, however weak) that arises with thinking or seeing or indeed with any kind of sensory experience.

What is generally referred to as an emotion is, in Buddhist terms, a feeling plus the subsequent response to that feeling. In other words, an emotion comprises both a resultant and an action. So where the man on the street talks about a feeling of rage, a meditator would label 'painful feeling' and 'anger'.

This is critically important. Painful feelings, being the result of past selfish action, are inevitable, unstoppable. On the other hand, actions (mental or physical) based in anger are optional.

Pleasant feelings are also inevitable. Suppose someone pays you a compliment. Hearing their words, you feel good. But if you then act on that feeling, if you respond with conceit and self-satisfaction, you are performing *kamma*. Such an action produces resultants - it produces future feelings and perceptions.

In the second noble truth the Buddha said that suffering has an origin and that its origin is craving, wanting things to be different. We tend to grasp at pleasurable feelings and seek to prolong them. We tend to push away painful feelings in our reluctance to experience them. Both these responses are based in craving, they are both *kamma*, they are both chosen.

Mind, especially in the early days of meditation, can seem somewhat amorphous. The meditator must learn to separate out the different components of mental experience. To overcome suffering, we have to learn the difference between feelings (which are simply resultants) and actions (volitional movements of mind rooted in craving, hatred and ignorance).

The pleasure experienced on hearing a particular piece of music is quite different from the urge to play it through again and again. The pleasure derived from a stimulating conversation is different from the incessant craving to talk.

The pain we may experience if unjustly accused is not the same as the resentment we may direct towards our accuser. A physical pain that might come up in the meditation is not the same as our misguided attempts to squirm away from it.

Gaining the ability to be mindful of feelings and subsequent responses as discrete and separate mental phenomena forms a real landmark in a meditator's practice. Now he understands that there is absolutely no need for him to do anything about his feelings - which comes as a real relief. Whether feelings are pleasant or painful, he knows they come and go independent of his wishes.

He further understands that he **is** responsible for his actions and that, if he restrains responses based in craving or hatred, he will not be setting himself up for more suffering for the future.

Testing Assumptions

Three people shortlisted for a new job hear they've been unsuccessful. The first person is angry: he **knows** he has been rejected because he's the wrong sex and the wrong colour. The second person, secure in her new age certainties, is not concerned; she sees the rejection as a sign that that avenue was not the right one for her, that life has something better in store. The third person is upset but not surprised – who would want to give **him** a job anyway?

A couple sit down in front of the television to watch the news. They watch reports of economic crises, serial killings, new divorce statistics. They shake their heads in disapproval – the world is going from bad to worse.

Unless we train ourselves to observe without prejudice, we tend to automatically select from the environment evidence which confirms our existing views.

In meditation we have to systematically direct our attention. If we try to just 'be aware', then – like the people watching the news – we merely corroborate what we already believe. If we do not specifically attend to transience, unsatisfactoriness and *anatta*, we will go on seeing things in terms of permanence, satisfactoriness and self. A meditator may attend to the rise and fall of the abdomen and yet, if he does not expressly direct his attention towards the transience of all aspects of the experience, there will be no change in the way he sees the world and therefore no change in his behaviour.

The Buddha stated that all conditioned things are transient, unsatisfactory and non-self. He also told people not to take any teaching on trust - his own included. However accurate a description of reality may be, if we do not know the truth for ourselves, it remains a description and only a description.

We each have to test the Buddha's teaching against our own experience. It is not enough simply to believe that things are transient - we have to investigate our experience and discover the fact of transience for ourselves.

A meditator has heard all about transience and yet he thinks that the pain in his shoulder is there to stay. He considers various options: he might indulge in self-pity; he might decide to force the mind on to the rise and fall to try and sidestep the pain, or veer off into fantasy. But he's tried these things before - he knows they just make it worse. So he approaches the pain meditatively. He does the last thing most people would ever consider: he simply observes.

What he discovers is that the pain is as ephemeral as any other object. If he tries to hold his mind on the pain, he finds that he cannot keep it there - it slides off on to sounds, thoughts or other sensory data. He realises that at that moment when the mind is engaged with these other objects the pain does not exist. He discovers that the solid, enduring block of pain was just a concept. In reality, he experiences a moment of physical sensation which rises and falls - then a painful feeling - then a thought, 'I can't stand an hour of this' - then perhaps a sound, another painful feeling and so on. Pain does not last - nothing lasts.

Investigation

The Buddha provided a clear and precise description of reality. If his description is to become personally meaningful, all of us have to test the truth of his words for ourselves. We each have to explore our own experience – can we find anything which is truly satisfactory, something unchanging that we can always rely on, something we can unfailingly control and possess?

Effective meditation is never ritualistic. It requires an inquisitive, investigative approach. Essentially, we have to investigate the three marks, but there are also other issues that need to be explored in the course of the training.

For example, many people believe that we can experience more than one thing at a time. When we come to meditation we are told that this is not the case. Rather than simply holding an opinion on the matter, we observe our experience with a view to finding out for ourselves what **actually** happens.

Investigation needs to be integrated with other factors such as mindfulness and concentration. When mindfulness and concentration are weak, it can **appear** as if events are concurrent – it can seem as if hearing and seeing, for example, take place simultaneously. When mindfulness and concentration are strong, it becomes obvious to the meditator that one moment there is hearing, the next there is seeing, the next there is thinking, and so on.

The mind's ability to flick rapidly from sense to sense suggests that things overlap and thus gives an illusion of continuity. In reality, in any one moment we can only be aware of one thing.

We also need to investigate such issues as the difference – in experiential terms – between mindfulness and concentration, or between mental energy and physical energy, or between actions based (however subtly) in self-concern and those free from craving.

While meditative investigation is not itself an intellectual process, the meditator does need to become familiar to some extent with the Buddha's description in order to direct the mind in the most effective manner. So a certain amount of intellectual work is imperative – reading books, attending classes or asking questions of teachers, thinking about and assimilating the information.

For those meditators who are inclined to fall back too easily on habitual assumptions, to read and to think about the teaching can inspire a more inquisitive approach in the meditation. Without an attitude of enquiry, the general tone of the practice tends to be dull and routine.

Too much investigation produces the opposite effect. The mind becomes restless and excitable, quite incapable of settling on the rise and fall. Unless this craving to find answers is tempered, the questions, the uncertainties, the doubts will proliferate endlessly.

Correct meditation produces insight but insights cannot be produced to order. None of us can know how much observation it will take before we make a link between a state of personal distress, for example, and the inefficient actions that conditioned that state; or before a clear insight into transience arises. Patience is crucial.

Most of us are at times tempted to try and speed up the process - to apply a little more energy, to probe into experience a little more deeply. When investigation is excessive, the meditator loses sight of the relevance of direct experience. He becomes tangled up in thinking, seeking answers through the apparent shortcut of intellectual reasoning.

Correct investigation is always directed at experience - not at our ideas about experience.

Faith

Many Westerners are attracted to Buddhism because of its rationality and lack of dogma. Unlike so many religious ways, Buddhism – it would seem – does not call for faith.

King Pasenadi once described to the Buddha how on one occasion, when he was on military manoeuvres, he observed the behaviour of two of his servants, Isidatta and Purana. They were up most of the night talking about the teaching and, when they did decide to sleep, they lay down with their heads directed towards where they believed the Buddha to be staying, their feet towards the king. Pasenadi was amazed – an absolute monarch was not used to coming second best.

An epithet the Buddha himself frequently applied to the teaching was *ehi-passiko* – come and see for yourself. And yet he also said that faith is one of the qualities that must be developed before real progress towards enlightenment is possible.

When we start off, none of us can know for sure that there is a solution to the problem of suffering. The very fact that we are looking for an answer at all indicates that we believe that one may exist. We wouldn't take up a path if we didn't think it would be of some benefit to us. But until we have some meditative experience of our own against which to test the Buddha's words, we have no option but to take them on trust. At this stage there are no guarantees.

It is only after having lived by the precepts for some time, for example, that a meditator begins to appreciate their significance. What started off as a willingness to try them out gradually evolves into confidence in their importance. He no longer just **believes** that the precepts are worth keeping – he knows it.

This illustrates the way faith is developed – through action, through putting the teaching into practice.

The meditator who has discovered the efficacy of the precepts has an increased confidence in the training as a whole. He is now ready to take on trust aspects of the teaching which previously he may have found difficult. If he is told, for example, that his periods of depression are actually self-chosen, he no longer resists the idea but is prepared to observe the whole area with an open mind.

Those whose faith is weak always want to know the answers before they commit themselves. As far as the meditative path is concerned, they're caught in a complete double-bind – they want assurance that the training works but they resist doing the only thing that can give them the answer.

We could spend years preparing intellectually – studying the Buddha's teachings in all their complexity – but, to know the truth for ourselves, we have at some point to start to practise. A man might know all there is to know about the chemical and physical properties of water but he will not understand what water really is until he jumps into the river.

Walking the path inevitably involves leaping into the unknown. Abandoning our habitual views and assumptions requires faith. But every time we move forward in this way, our confidence and trust in the path increases.

The Buddha said that our problems are caused by craving, which is itself based on an ignorance of the way things are. Get rid of the ignorance and the problems disappear forever. Over the centuries, countless men and women have realised for themselves the truth of his words. In the face of such a compellingly positive vision, is there any valid reason not to give it a try?

A Positive World-view

As far as many people are concerned, the universe is not a benevolent place. They believe that if they drop their guard someone is likely to take advantage of them. Given such an outlook, distrust and self-interest inevitably predominate, along with a tendency to home in automatically on the negative side of situations and people – oneself included.

Such jaundiced views are always destructive of the attempt to pay objective attention. For anyone who is prone to such thoughts – and who has not at times indulged in thinking of this kind? – it is necessary to employ specific measures to redress the balance.

One of the most important practices in this respect is *metta* or loving-kindness meditation. In essence, *metta* is the desire for the welfare and happiness of all beings. The purpose of *metta* meditation is to counteract an habitually critical mind-set by focusing systematically on the positive qualities that all beings have. Practising *metta* on a regular basis produces a mind which is warm, open and accepting.

An inevitable consequence of developing a positive outlook through *metta* is that other beings respond in kind. We are all inter-related; whether consciously or not, we recognise and are influenced by the mental states of those around us. If we ourselves are feeling cheerful and optimistic, we will tend to attract a similarly positive response. Furthermore, it is said that those committed to the practice of *metta* are dear both to human beings and to non-human beings and that they are protected from 'fire, poison, sword and stick'.

Another benefit of *metta* is that sleep comes easily and is not disturbed by anxiety dreams or nightmares. Moreover, someone who has developed *metta* is likely, it is said, to die peacefully and, thanks to their positive mental actions, to be reborn into favourable circumstances.

In a world where conflict and dissension are commonplace, developing a mind filled with *metta* is undoubtedly one of the most positive actions it is possible to undertake. Dedication to the practice brings inestimable benefits, transforming one's whole outlook on life. Positive qualities - such as kindness, co-operation, generosity and compassion - now are seen as natural human traits instead of idealistic aberrations.

But *metta*, no matter how highly developed, can never lead to the end of suffering. However beneficial the results of *metta* practice - both to the individual and to those with whom he or she comes into contact - they cannot last indefinitely and they cannot themselves lead to enlightenment.

Metta does, however, provide the perfect complement to *vipassana* meditation. The openness and pliancy of mind generated by the practice of loving-kindness forms an ideal basis for the development of systematic observation.

Another quality of mind intimately connected with *metta* is patience. And so the cultivation of *metta* has the further advantage of tempering the driving ambition and goal-orientation which, for many of us, can cause such obstruction to the *vipassana* practice.

For any *vipassana* meditator who ever finds him- or herself troubled by fault-finding, by impatience, by ambition, by resentment, by negativity generally, *metta* is not an optional extra – it is an indispensable necessity.

The Practice of Metta

Throughout recorded history philosophers and religious teachers have emphasised the profound importance of love. Buddhism is striking in that it actually provides a clear and systematic guide on how to develop it.

Like *vipassana*, *metta* is practised as a formal meditation – sitting on a chair with the eyes closed. The practice involves several distinct stages.

The first step entails recollecting – that is, consciously thinking about – the disadvantages of hatred. For example, the meditator might call to mind an occasion when he or she had failed to restrain anger and remember just how destructive such indulgence had been. Or, he might consider how alienating hatred is – no one wants to have anything to do with someone whose mind is full of resentment and bitterness.

Next, the meditator needs to review the advantages of *metta*, as outlined in the previous chapter.

These two stages need not take more than a few minutes but they are essential. They introduce a clarity of purpose and enthuse the mind for the practice.

In the third stage, the meditator develops thoughts of loving-kindness towards him- or herself. In many cases, this is undoubtedly the most difficult aspect of the practice. So many people resist the idea that they are worthy of their own affection. This seems to be one of the major disadvantages of our western conditioning. But unless the meditator is as happy developing *metta* towards himself as he is to others, the practice can never properly succeed.

To generate a feeling of warmth towards himself, the meditator thinks about his own positive qualities. This is in many ways the essence of *metta*. Just as hatred seeks out and focuses on the negative, so in developing loving-kindness we are counteracting that bias by training ourselves to seek out the positive. And all beings and situations **do** have a positive side.

A meditator, for example, might consider his generosity, his patience, his honesty, the fact that he has attempted to live by the precepts for a long period of time. He might also choose to see himself happy and relaxed. Such visualisations are a great aid in the development of *metta*, although it is the friendliness generated that is all-important.

Now, in the fourth stage, the meditator can work on developing *metta* towards others.

Traditionally, he begins with a person he respects, such as a teacher - someone he admires but to whom he is not particularly close. Again, he recollects their positive qualities, visualises them smiling and happy and wishes them well. Next he repeats the process towards a person he **is** close to, followed by someone towards whom he has no strong feelings either way. Finally, he develops *metta* towards someone he dislikes.

Obviously, it is more difficult to generate feelings of friendliness towards a person to whom one feels antagonistic and yet, with systematic application, it is entirely possible. The full development of the practice is traditionally described as 'breaking down the barriers' - where the meditator regards **all** beings, himself included, as equally worthy of *metta*.

The fourth stage - developing *metta* towards others - can take a variety of forms. For example, we might choose to focus on specific groups of beings, such as all opticians, all Australians, all seagulls ... Or we might practise *metta* towards all the beings to the north, to the south, to the east, to the west, above and below.

In another technique the meditator, having reviewed the disadvantages of hatred and the advantages of *metta*, visualises a candle-flame in the region of the solar plexus. As he develops loving-kindness towards himself, he visualises this flame increasing in size until he can see himself sitting within it. He then extends this flame of *metta* further so that it fills the entire room; he wishes that all beings within that area be well and happy. He extends the flame further yet - to fill the whole building, the street, the town, the country ... At each step, he develops friendliness to all beings within the flame - humans, animals, insects, those in other realms.

He completes the practice by contracting the flame through the same series of steps until it is returned to the solar plexus.

Typically, a meditator spends the first ten or fifteen minutes of his daily session of formal practice developing loving-kindness. Alternatively, he may be instructed to practise *vipassana* exclusively for one session, *metta* for the next.

As with all types of meditation, the practice works best when the mind is bright and interested. *Metta* meditation relies on the use of imagination and creativity but, whatever technique is employed, it is important to remember that it is the loving-kindness itself that counts – the specific techniques used to develop it are always subsidiary.

Anyone who practises *metta* on a regular basis finds that not only are his relationships transformed but the quality of life as a whole is enriched.

As well as counteracting hatred, *metta* also enhances the ability to concentrate. As such, it is a practice which, in the last analysis, the *vipassana* meditator cannot do without.

Insight

Insight meditation is very simple. Essentially we turn the mind time and time again to the transience of all mental and physical phenomena. This process culminates in a moment of insight.

An insight is an intuitive recognition of the true nature of things. In the context of *vipassana* practice, this means seeing at an experiential level one of the three marks – transience, unsatisfactoriness or non-self.

Such insights are completely non-intellectual; they are the result of repeated meditative observation, not of thought or speculation. However strongly someone might have **believed** he knew things were transient, it is only through direct insight that he truly knows it to be the case.

Meditation may be simple but it is not easy. *Vipassana* itself is straightforward but we obscure its essential simplicity with the complications we all bring to the practice. We have to learn to pay attention to transience for its own sake – not for what I can get out of it. We have to learn to pay attention to transience – not to our ideas about transience. We have to learn to get out of the way and not interfere with the natural intelligence of the mind.

The meditator's task is simply to gather data - repeatedly noting that everything he becomes aware of is transient. It is mind itself that produces insight, as a completely impersonal function.

The development of insight cannot be hurried. Basically, when a sufficient number of observations have been made, insight will arise. Self-involvement - in the form, for example, of impatience, frustration or a passionate desire for results - is always completely counterproductive.

Because our ignorance of transience is so ingrained, it takes more than a single insight to overcome it. Over months and years of dedicated application to the practice, many insights can arise. They will vary in intensity and can happen at any time - they certainly aren't restricted to the formal seated practice.

Insight arises through the simple observation of the three marks - if the practice seems complicated we are doing it wrong.

Making Mistakes

In learning any skill, making mistakes is an integral and completely unavoidable part of the process. Meditation is no exception.

The degree of mental precision required to pay alert unbiased attention should not be underestimated. Further, enlightenment **is** the unknown. Following the Buddha's path, we inevitably move into uncharted territory – areas of mind of which we have no experience. It is hardly surprising that there are times when we get it wrong. In fact, one teacher has described meditation as 'learning what **not** to do'.

Once we appreciate that it is actually only by making mistakes that we learn, we can relax. Mistakes are then seen not as some kind of failure which reflects on us personally but as opportunities to refine our approach.

What is vital is that we are honest with ourselves. In order to progress, it is essential that we acknowledge exactly what is going on in the practice. For example, a meditator may convince himself that everything is going well, when in fact most of the time he is lost in daydreams. He manages completely to overlook the fact that he can't hold his attention on the feeling of the rise and fall for more than a couple of counts. Until he is able to accept the true state of affairs, his practice will not go anywhere.

If, however, he admits to himself that he is not getting it right - and if he also talks to his teacher about the problem - he can do something about it. The teacher then has the opportunity to suggest the best approach for getting the practice moving again.

Or suppose a woman has a quick temper and often ends up saying things she later regrets. Because she is serious about keeping the precepts, whenever this happens she feels perfectly justified in launching into a bout of self-recrimination. Over time, she comes to recognise that this response is completely counterproductive - when the mind is filled with self-criticism, meditation is impossible. Knowing now through experience that self-recrimination only increases suffering, she abandons it. She learns through her mistake.

The Buddha's path gives clear guidelines on matters of ethical behaviour and on how to meditate. It does not, however, provide us with a rule for every occasion. There are always going to be times when we don't know how best to act. From a conventional standpoint, whatever course of action we choose may turn out to be mistaken. But as long as we act with mindfulness, we cannot help but gain wisdom. And in that case was the mistake a mistake?

Sense-restraint

What is most people's idea of happiness? Pleasure - food, sex, music, films, clothes, holidays, conversation. The chase for sensory pleasure is the main driving force behind the wheel of birth and death. Craving for pleasure, we are born, we grow old, we die - we suffer.

The Buddha made it clear that true happiness cannot be found through sense-pleasures. Someone hearing the Buddha's message may well recognise the truth of his words, but it is one thing to believe that sense-pleasures are inherently flawed and quite another to be able to drop our habitual preoccupation with them.

Craving fills the mind with chatter. We become obsessed with what we want and how we are going to get it. A mind caught up with such insistent activity does not have the poise or detachment necessary for the development of mindfulness and concentration. Therefore, if we want to meditate successfully, we have to learn to restrain our involvement with sensory information.

A meditator is attempting to be mindful of body while ironing some clothes. He intends to pay attention to all the physical movements involved but he also wants to catch a current affairs programme on the radio. All he succeeds in doing is setting up a lot of tension in the mind. He doesn't make a particularly good job of the ironing, he can't really follow the programme and he never really remembers to be mindful.

A meditator is attempting to be mindful of body while walking through town. She also wants to look in the shop-windows. After a few minutes, her mind is filled with images of the things she would like to buy, how she's going to pay for them, what she's going to do with them.

If the first meditator had simply switched the radio off, if the second meditator had refused to let her eyes roam over window-displays, their attempts to practise mindfulness would have been more successful. This control of the physical senses is the first level of sense-restraint.

The second level is the restraint of the mind itself. It is all very well refusing to look in a window but, unless this restraint is accompanied by a resolve not to think about the things that might be in the window and how much you might want them, it's of limited value. We have to keep turning the mind away from fantasy and speculation, from the self-involvement which is so destructive of the attempt to be mindful.

The essence of sense-restraint is the pragmatic control of the range of our senses - mind included - for the express purpose of enhancing mindfulness.

Sense-restraint is **not** moralistic. There is nothing ethically wrong with listening to the radio at the same time as doing the ironing. It's just that it doesn't help us on the path to enlightenment.

Many people, when they first hear about sense-restraint, respond rather negatively. They believe that restricting their senses will impoverish their experience. If they give it a try, they find it actually does the opposite.

Although sense-restraint entails giving up some short-term pleasure, it helps create the best conditions for the development of concentration, mindfulness and insight. (And, paradoxically, the meditator who restrains his senses discovers that a quieter mind is actually more pleasurable.)

We can, in fact, never get rid of sense-pleasures, just as we can never get rid of pain. As long as we've got senses, we're going to experience pleasure and pain. They are not the problem. The problem is the craving to indulge in pleasure and to avoid pain.

Although craving can never be overcome by control alone, without sense-restraint enlightenment is not possible.

The Worldly Conditions

There are, according to Buddhist tradition, eight 'worldly conditions' – ubiquitous and unavoidable – which characterise our life in the human realm. These are grouped into four pairs, namely: pleasure and pain, gain and loss, praise and blame, fame and obscurity.

The way of the world is to attempt to manipulate our circumstances so that we only experience what we regard as positive. Emotionally, we act as if it were possible to exclude all pain and loss while experiencing a continuous stream of pleasure and material gain.

Meditation doesn't change the world. Even the enlightened person is subject to these four pairs of conditions. Through meditation we learn to accept the inevitability of these changing circumstances. We see more and more clearly that they **are** transient – pleasure can be interrupted at any moment by the arising of pain, and vice versa.

The more we understand the inevitability and transience of these conditions, the less we are attached to them.

The usual response to an unexpected legacy, for example, is elation; the usual response to redundancy is despair. Because of people's identification with the eight conditions, responses in such circumstances tend to be extreme. Another word for identification is attachment. Where there is attachment, there is anxiety and fear - a desperation to hold on to what we've got and a desire to keep at bay anything that threatens our comfort and security. We can be mistrustful, restless, aggressive.

The trained meditator, however, does not centre his life around gain, loss, praise, etc, and is not psychologically thrown by changing fortunes. He regards life's vicissitudes not in terms of personal profit but as opportunities for learning about the true nature of reality.

Conventional & Ultimate Truth

A novice put to one side a bowl that was smeared with oil. When it was time to drink gruel, an elder told him to bring him the bowl. He said, 'But venerable sir, there is oil in it.' Later, the elder said, 'Bring me that bowl of oil and I'll fill up this oil-tube.' To which the novice replied, 'But it's empty, venerable sir.'

This passage from an ancient Buddhist text illustrates the relativity of truth. As a drinking vessel, the bowl contained oil and so was unfit for use; yet as an oil-container, it was to all intents and purposes empty.

What is true in one situation is not necessarily true in another. To a child, for example, a thousand pounds is a fortune; when he grows up to be a barrister, it's pocket money.

A statement may be true but, to avoid confusion and misunderstanding, we need to know in what context it's true. The top footballer in a local team, for example, may be regarded as a real star; put him with international-class players and he turns out to be an embarrassment.

In Buddhism two specific kinds of truth are distinguished. The first kind - conventional truth - deals with the world of technology, the environment, careers, art, families, countries and politics; it deals with beings – their births, lives and deaths, both in the human realm and elsewhere.

At the level of the second kind of truth – ultimate truth – none of these things exists. Ultimate truth is solely concerned with moment-to-moment sense data, with the very building-blocks from which we create our ideas of the world.

At the conventional level, we might say we see a car. At the ultimate level, there is simply the experiencing of shape and colour – at this level, a 'car' is simply a concept.

Someone says he's got a headache – that's true at the conventional level. If he were speaking in ultimate terms, he would say there is pressure, temperature, feeling.

At the conventional level, we might get highly indignant if we are unjustly accused. At the ultimate level, there is the experience of hearing, then perception, painful feeling and self-concerned mental action. At the ultimate level there are no beings – no accuser, no one to be accused. There is just a momentary succession of irreducible mental and physical phenomena.

Although transience **is** observable at the conventional level, *vipassana* meditation requires the greater precision of the ultimate level.

Someone might start thinking about the onset of winter and find himself morosely counting the long months ahead before his next annual holiday. He is aware of the changing seasons and, to that extent, he is aware of transience. But at this very general level it makes little or no difference to the way he behaves. It is the observation of the transience of ultimates which transforms our lives.

A meditator finds herself thinking about the onset of winter. She's had the presence of mind to realise that the train of thought was prompted by the sight of the colours of the leaves. She notes 'seeing', arising and ceasing in the moment; she notes the subsequent perception, 'It's autumn'. A pleasant feeling arises – she likes this time of year. That ceases and a thought arises about how long it's going to be before she can take any time off work. That thought is followed by an unpleasant feeling. The feeling in turn is followed by a moment when she sees that she **could** grasp at that feeling and then descend into self-pity.

But she knows through painful experience just how futile such actions are. She notes that the urge to grasp has dissolved. Rather than choosing the claustrophobia of a depressive fantasy, she remains attentive and alert, alive to the moment-by-moment unfolding of reality.

Through meditation we find that no matter how closely we look at our experience all we find is a succession of the most fleeting moments of mental and physical phenomena. Things are seen to be so ephemeral that our old ideas about permanence and continuity are no longer tenable. And without views of permanence and continuity, craving and hatred are not possible.

Anatta

To human society, permanence, satisfactoriness and the existence of a self are self-evident truths. The Buddha said that these views are quite wrong and, further, that they lead to all the misery and distress in the world. He said that in reality **all** things are subject to the three marks of *anicca*, *dukkha* and *anatta* – transience, unsatisfactoriness and non-self. This statement is extremely challenging.

We resist the fact that unsatisfactoriness is inherent in all things – after all, we couldn't crave for things if we didn't believe them to be satisfactory.

We might concede, though, that nothing lasts – which means that we can appreciate (intellectually at least) that nothing can be **really** satisfactory.

What really causes problems, however, what people find most challenging, is the concept of *anatta*.

Anatta literally translates as 'non-self'. When the Buddha said things were *anatta*, he meant that nowhere in the world is there such a thing as a lasting independent entity. Nothing contains an enduring essence; nothing has a soul or self.

When we use a term like 'tree', 'building' or 'computer', we tend to assume that the word refers to a real separate object. When we look more closely, however, we see that in reality all there is is a combination of transient conditions.

What we call a tree, for example, is actually a collection of different physical structures, each of which is itself in a process of constant flux. If you take away the leaves, the branches, the trunk and roots, no tree remains. It has no identity independent of its component parts.

Further, a tree is completely dependent for its existence on an appropriate environment - light, soil, moisture, nutrients, warmth, etc. Remove any one of these conditions and the tree dies. All things are interdependent - nothing stands alone.

Everything in the physical world is *anatta* - everything in the mental world is *anatta*. Bodies are *anatta*, minds are *anatta*, personalities are *anatta*.

We are conditioned to believe that we each have a personality which should remain more or less consistent, regardless of prevailing circumstances. And yet, if we take a closer look, we see that we are chameleons - we are constantly changing.

Most noticeably, our personalities vary according to who we're with. With some people we are warm and expansive. With others we tend to be self-conscious and lacking in confidence. Some people bring out our authoritarian streak, while with our parents we might behave like eight-year-olds.

Our personalities - like every other aspect of our minds and bodies - are conditioned by our past actions and by the circumstances we find ourselves in now. We change with the weather, the state of our health, our age, the amount of stress we're under, the amount of attention we receive ... We change with every new experience. There is **nothing** within us that remains the same.

On hearing that the Buddha denied the existence of a self or soul, some people believe that they have found an inconsistency within his teaching. If we have no self, they argue, what is it that gets reborn?

At the conventional level, there is continuity. I existed yesterday, I exist today and, all things being equal, I shall exist tomorrow. At the ultimate level, there is just the momentary arising of mental and physical objects - there are no beings, no selves, no entities. This ultimate level does not negate the conventional level and vice versa - they are just different modes of analysis. Whenever we try to mix these levels, problems are bound to ensue.

Consider a chair. At one level it is a solid structure - a wooden frame, an upholstered seat. At another level, it is a combination of sub-atomic particles. Both these levels are true. But one would be foolish to believe the chair would be uncomfortable because all the particles are in motion. To avoid confusion, we have to be clear about what level we're dealing with.

Anatta 2

A woman is sitting on a roadside bench waiting for a friend. She is whiling away the time idly watching the cars going up and down the road. She sits there quite happily for five or ten minutes – and then her tranquillity is shattered and she starts to panic. The car now disappearing into the distance, she suddenly realises, is hers.

Self-view causes countless problems. As soon as we identify with anything, as soon as we grasp at anything as me or mine, we have something to lose, something to control, something to defend, something to worry about.

Whenever we see things in terms of self, whenever we believe in the absolute reality of 'me myself', we obstruct the flow of life. In creating 'self' we automatically create 'other'. Assuming ourselves to be concrete entities we find ourselves inhabiting a world of dependency, demand, claustrophobia, a world of 'control or be controlled'.

A man is sitting on a train engrossed in a book. He is not particularly aware of his surroundings until a flurry of movement alerts him to the fact that someone has sat down in the opposite seat. Glancing up, he sees an attractive young woman. Instantly he is aware of himself in relationship to her. His sense of settledness and ease is gone. His mind starts racing with thoughts about how he looks, what he might say, has she noticed him. He is agitated, self-conscious, uncomfortable.

It is only because of ignorance of the way things truly are that anyone can believe in a separate self. The Buddha's path reverses all ignorance, totally destroying the very basis of self-view.

Vipassana meditation is not static. Although the technique remains the same, over time the practice transforms and develops. And it is a sign of correct application that it **does** change - these changes are a natural outcome of the observation of transience.

There is a stage in the practice where the meditator becomes increasingly aware that sensory experience only arises when the appropriate conditions are present. In technical Buddhist terms, he sees that consciousness only arises dependent on the presence of a sense-object and a functioning sense-base. In everyday English, hearing cannot occur unless there is a sound to be heard and an ear to hear it.

This may seem obvious enough theoretically, but at this point the meditator **knows** through direct experience that hearing is a conditioned process and completely impersonal. He sees that it is a transient event that arises dependent on equally transient conditions - no self is necessary.

This realisation is the first major insight into *anatta*. The more we see that all experience is impersonal - that all there is is a succession of mental and physical events, all of them selfless, transient, unownable, uncontrollable - the more our belief in self is eroded.

Many resist the idea of *anatta* because they fear they will lose something. They imagine that meditation destroys something that actually exists. But self never has existed. All that meditation destroys is wrong ideas.

Attachment To View

It is not unknown for a meditator to assume that, simply by virtue of the fact that he is following a spiritual path, he is no longer prey to such states as anger, envy, depression. If he is strongly attached to this view, he has no option but to ignore all evidence to the contrary.

Success in meditation depends upon an open mind. We have to be willing to examine whatever arises - correct *vipassana* practice is free of all internal censorship. If there is any aspect of our mental or physical experience that we refuse to acknowledge, meditation becomes predictable, sterile, lifeless. Repression also tends to make us feel increasingly estranged from our fellow beings.

One of the major obstacles to meditative progress is attachment to views, opinions, beliefs. A meditator may be attached to a view of himself, as being perceptive or confused or sophisticated or advanced. He may be attached to a political ideology, to a theory of psychoanalysis, to his views on relationships or technology or music or abortion. He may be attached to a particular self-image based on his gender, his nationality, his ethnic background, his level of education, his skills.

A college-educated European was staying in a remote tribal village in India. One night conversation turned to the stars. He realised that the local people all believed that the earth was flat. He tried to put them right. It was obvious they thought his ideas were ludicrous. He got increasingly frustrated at what he saw as their rejection of his attempts to share his knowledge.

The tribal people held a view that was factually incorrect. The European's view of astronomy was scientifically accurate. The tribal people were quite happy with their view – it didn't make them suffer in any way. The European, however, **was** suffering – his attachment to his view ensured that.

Attachment to **any** view is a problem. A Buddhist academic might sincerely believe that anyone who follows the Buddha's path will find the quality of their life dramatically improves. So far so good. If, however, he gets passionately involved with what is for him, after all, only an idea, he becomes prejudiced, defensive, contentious.

A woman hears that her aged mother has died. After the initial shock, she is surprised to find that she feels very little. Influenced by a lifetime of cultural conditioning and the social pressure she now feels herself under, she picks up a view: 'You should feel devastated at the death of a parent'. She identifies with the view, she repeatedly grasps at it, she turns the thoughts over and over in mind. The result of this attachment is tremendous guilt – her cool response to her mother's death does not conform with the way she believes she **should** respond.

How is attachment to view overcome? Firstly, we need to become aware of the presence of our views – this is something that gradually happens as a natural consequence of practising mindfulness. We also need to be clear that a view is simply a view - one specific interpretation out of a potentially infinite number of interpretations.

Our views are conditioned. We incline towards certain views based on our past experience. Our views are conditioned by the actions we've made, our upbringing, our education, the values of the culture we live in.

If someone has been brought up in Japan, for example, she is likely to be shocked the first time she sees a westerner enter a house without taking off his shoes.

Most people who've had a western liberal education take it for granted that arranged marriages are a bad thing. To many in traditional oriental societies, however, a marriage based purely in romantic attraction is asking for trouble.

Every time we choose to see the world in a specific way, we strengthen our inclination towards that view. If, for example, we practise *metta* (loving-kindness) regularly, we actually **see** people as being far more likeable. As the Buddha said, 'Whatever the meditator ponders and reflects on much, the mind in consequence gets a bias that way.'

Because of our past, our personality, our circumstances, certain views are going to arise in the moment. We can't help it. But we don't have to grasp at them. We can instead see them for what they are - transient, conditioned, arbitrary. This doesn't mean that we won't have views - we'll still have opinions, maybe even strong opinions - but we won't be attached to them.

Our views, no matter how proud, possessive or passionate we are about them, are *anatta*. In the traditional wording, they are 'not me, not mine, not the self of me'.

Diet

Food is central to human experience. As such it frequently becomes the focus of passionate attachment. Many find it easy to be indulgent, neurotic or ascetic about food and diet. In fact, in many ways our attitude to food mirrors our attitude towards all sense-pleasures.

As with all areas of life, the meditator needs to find a middle way, avoiding the dietary extremes which exacerbate self-concern and attachment to view.

When the Buddha established the monastic orders, he set them up so that the monks and nuns were totally dependent on the lay community for their food. Basically, whatever people cared to give, the monks and nuns were obliged to eat. Any views they might hold about what they should or should not eat had to be put to one side.

This approach necessitates the relinquishing of attachment - relinquishing attachment frees the mind.

Some meditators might object, believing it more important to avoid cholesterol, sugar, wheat products, meat, caffeine. Certainly, where possible, it is sensible to maintain a healthy diet but, in the final analysis, the body is *dukkha* - its nature is to decay and die. It cannot last however much we might pamper and protect it. Over-concern with diet is indicative of attachment to body - a belief that the body could be permanent and satisfactory. Such attachment to view chains us to the wheel of birth and death.

There are, on the other hand, those whose indifference to the body goes too far - they fall into another extreme. These are the ascetics who pride themselves on their self-denial and control, who believe that fasting has some inherent spiritual significance. For such people establishing a middle way involves actually taking more care of their health and diet.

The Buddha emphasised the importance of the correct meditative attitude towards food, singling out an understanding of 'moderation in eating' as a specific stage in the training. A meditator who has learned to be moderate regards food essentially as fuel. Rather than seeing it as primarily a source of pleasure or comfort, he recognises that, for anyone working on the path to enlightenment, the true purpose of food is simply to keep the body functioning and reasonably healthy.

Thinking

To many, meditation means emptying the mind - stopping thinking. Anyone who really believes this is going to find the practice of meditation very difficult indeed.

The essence of *vipassana* meditation, as we have seen, is observation - not manipulation. Thinking is natural. It is as natural for the mind to experience thoughts as it is for it to experience sights or sounds.

A meditator comes-to and realises he has spent the last quarter of an hour lost in a train of thought. His immediate response is one of hatred - he sees the thinking as robbing him of the opportunity to make meditative progress. He swings from one extreme - passionate involvement with the flow of ideas - to another - desire to destroy the whole process of thinking.

As with all aspects of experience, there is a middle way. The meditator has to learn how to acknowledge the presence of thoughts without either getting caught up in them or reacting passionately against them.

We have to train ourselves to attend not to the content or story-line of our thoughts but rather to the process of thinking.

Two people are meditating together. Suddenly, a car alarm goes off. The first meditator launches straight into self-concerned thoughts, wondering if it's his car, what he's going to do about it, is his insurance up to date, should he stop meditating and go and investigate ...

The second meditator has the presence of mind to note the perception 'car alarm' and an urge to start worrying. He is aware that thoughts are arising; he is aware that they are triggered by the sound of the car alarm; he is aware that the sound is transient and the thoughts are transient. He knows that he could at any point pick up one of these thoughts and develop it, turn it round in mind – believe it.

The first meditator identifies with the content of his thinking. He allows himself to be sucked into the story-line, with the result that very soon he becomes distressed and completely loses track of meditation.

The second meditator remains mindful. He sees that the thoughts are conditioned. He knows that the perception 'car alarm' arose on a sound – without the sound there would have been no perception. He knows that the tendency to worry only arose because of past action – it arose because he has acted that way in the past. He remembers that he does not have to identify with any aspect of the process; the sound, the perception, the feelings, the thoughts – they're all impersonal, all 'not me', 'not mine'. He calmly continues to observe the unfolding events, grasping at nothing. He continues to meditate.

Thoughts are just another aspect of sensory experience. They are no better, no worse than sights or sounds or physical contacts. Ultimately, their only significance to the *vipassana* meditator is the fact that they are *anicca, dukkha, anatta*.

Hindrances

In theory, *vipassana* meditation is simple. Indeed, the correct practice of *vipassana* is simplicity itself. Essentially, all complications and difficulties with the practice are based in self-concern.

The Buddha identified five major types of self-concerned thinking which can prove a real obstacle in meditation. These are five different aspects of grasping, five different manifestations of selfishness. They are known as the five hindrances and traditionally they are listed as sense-desire, ill-will, sloth and torpor, worry and restlessness, and doubt.

They are called hindrances because they hinder our ability to pay attention. When any of them is present in mind, it is not possible to see clearly.

No matter how tempting it might be to believe otherwise, the hindrances are always volitional - they are things we do.

Ideally, as soon as we recognise that we are indulging in self-concern - in other words, doing a hindrance - we stop doing it. In practical terms, however, dealing with the hindrances is not always this easy. For one thing, these actions can be so habitual, so automatic that, until we take up meditative training, we often have no idea that we are doing them. And even when we start becoming aware of our habitual modes of self-centredness, we are sometimes reluctant to let go of them.

Newcomers sometimes fall into the trap of thinking that these mental actions get in the way of real meditation. And yet, although learning to identify and overcome hindrances is not glamorous, it is central to the practice; it is a critically important aspect of *vipassana* which cannot be bypassed. Without a full experiential understanding of the hindrances, enlightenment is not possible.

Learning to deal with the hindrances is a gradual process. It can be hard work but it leads to a taste of a mental freedom quite independent of external conditions. Once a meditator has gained the ability to put aside the hindrances more or less at will, he is in the optimum position to deepen insight into transience and so make real progress towards *nibbana*.

In the next five chapters we will look at the hindrances in more detail.

Sense-desire

A man sits down to meditate. He's had a difficult day at work; he's tired and hungry. He never really gets on to the rise and fall because he spends the whole session dreaming about the meal he's going to eat when he's finished. What he wants is a mouthful of pizza - what he's got is another twenty minutes of sitting motionless on a chair with his eyes closed.

A woman is listening to a CD she's borrowed from a friend. It's an enjoyable enough experience but it could be better - what would make it better would be **owning** the CD. She decides she's got to go out and buy her own copy. Until she has, she's just not going to feel comfortable.

The whole of human experience is composed of individual moments of sensory contact - sights, sounds, smells, tastes, touches, thoughts. None of these things is a problem - problems only arise when we grasp after them. Whenever we decide that our current sensory experience is not good enough, that it should be replaced with something more satisfying, something more stimulating, then the hindrance of sense-desire is present.

If a meditator is planning his next holiday, or trying to induce some kind of visionary experience, or indulging in a sexual fantasy, or thinking about ending the meditation early so he can go and sit in the sun, he is doing sense-desire. Whenever sense-desire - or indeed any of the hindrances - fills the mind, it is not possible to successfully pay attention to the three marks. The mind is unsettled and is interested only in turning towards the object of its desire.

While it is true that the hindrances can only be finally eradicated by insight, the very presence of a hindrance prevents the clear seeing that is essential for insight to arise. Therefore the meditator needs to undertake certain strategies designed to keep the hindrances at bay.

Each of the five hindrances can be combated by specific counteractive measures. The most direct strategy for dealing with sense-desire is sense-restraint, refusing to allow the mind to linger over potentially problematic sensory contacts. For example, a trained meditator who loves computers might avoid looking up the specifications of the latest hardware if he knows that at present he can't afford to buy. He is tempted, but he is well aware that exposing himself to that kind of information will only lead to discontent.

Some people fall into the trap of believing that sense-desire could be eradicated altogether by isolating themselves completely from the objects they crave for. They mistakenly believe that it's the objects that cause the problems - not their attachment to them. Such people may conclude that they ought to deny themselves every possible form of pleasure. But pleasure - like pain - **cannot** be avoided; it is an inevitable and integral part of human experience. Pleasure will arise and, whenever a pleasurable feeling is present, there is the potential for the hindrance of sense-desire.

When we really want something, all we see are its advantages, its positive qualities. And so a particularly effective technique for countering sense-desire is to systematically bring to mind the faults and disadvantages of whatever it is we're getting so obsessive about.

A man living in a basement flat in central London starts thinking about how much better life would be if he could only get himself a place in the country. He sees himself living in a remote cottage in Wales - clean air, birdsong, organic vegetable garden. Every time life in the city seems too stressful he retreats into his daydream.

There comes a point when he realises that all this fantasising is just making him more unhappy. He starts to think about the reality of moving to the country - he probably wouldn't be able to find a job; he'd lose most of his friends; he'd miss the cultural life of the capital, the 24-hour shops, the restaurants. In fact, the countryside wouldn't really suit him at all.

The more he thinks along these lines, the more his mind settles. The fantasy doesn't interest him any more. He stops resenting the conditions of his life. He's a lot happier.

Reviewing the disadvantages of what we crave for may well be the last thing we'd want to do - after all, the hindrances are by their very nature seductive - but it does work. It reverses the very ignorance upon which the hindrances are based.

In addition to this technique, there are also various long-term strategies which are extremely useful in combating sense-desire.

Moderation in food, for example, is important - successfully restraining the craving for food makes it easier to restrain cravings for other sensory objects. Keeping the precepts is crucial - controlling our physical behaviour gives us the strength of purpose we need if we are to successfully restrain indulgence on the mental level.

Learning to concentrate allows us to remain aloof from sensory concerns; the deeper the level of concentration, the greater the degree of detachment.

These strategies can help enormously – but only when used in conjunction with the development of systematic mindfulness. In learning to overcome any of the hindrances, mindfulness is the most important single factor. Without mindful awareness of the presence of a hindrance, it is not possible to give it up.

In the eyes of the world, giving up sense-desire is madness. But what we find whenever we do succeed in relinquishing it is an experience of freedom which cannot be attained in any other way.

Ill-will

It's time to meditate. You can't really be bothered - you'd much rather stay slumped in front of the television. But you force yourself anyway.

The mind starts picking at thoughts about the futility of it all - you don't know why you're meditating, it never seems to go anywhere, it's just a lot of hard work. You drift off into thinking about an argument you had earlier in the day; you re-play the situation feeling more and more aggrieved and self-righteous. Then you remember you're meant to be meditating. You can't be bothered.

This is the hindrance of ill-will - it can't see anything good about anything. Just as sense-desire can only see the positive aspects of whatever it wants, ill-will can only see faults, problems, disadvantages. When ill-will is present in the mind, we criticise, we complain, we get irritable, angry, resentful.

Like all the hindrances, ill-will can cover a whole spectrum, from mild irritability to murderous rage. Like all the hindrances, ill-will is always volitional. Nothing in this world can make us angry - anger, resentment, ill-will are **always** chosen. Our interactions with others, for example, may give rise to unpleasant feelings, perhaps extremely painful ones. But the anger that is performed in response to pain never 'just happens' - it is not automatic, it is *kamma*, chosen action. Because ill-will is something we choose, it is always possible to choose not to do it.

As with sense-desire, there are specific strategies that can be employed to overcome this hindrance.

One common characteristic of a mind filled with ill-will is apathy. This can be directly countered by developing an interest in whatever is going on. If you're feeling fed up at work, for example, you could try questioning a colleague about some task they're engaged in. If you're fed up when you're meditating, you can decide to take an interest in the apathy itself - it's quite possible to get interested in the fact that the meditation does not seem interesting. Interest and apathy - interest and ill-will - cannot co-exist in the mind.

An effective means of encouraging oneself to restrain resentment and irritability is to bring to mind the inevitable consequences of indulging such thinking - troublesome relationships, for example, loss of reputation, a sense of shame and/or emotional exhaustion. Ill-will can do real damage to the environment and the beings in it - it is always most destructive to the person doing it.

For a meditator, ill-will is never justified. This includes ill-will towards oneself. It might be culturally acceptable in the West to indulge in self-hatred but from a meditative point of view self-hatred is just as bad as hatred of others.

In the long term, dedication to the practice of *metta* can have a marked effect on the general level of irritability or hatred in the mind. By training oneself to seek out the positive qualities of people and situations, one's inclination to focus on faults and imperfections tends to atrophy.

Boredom, depression, resentment, self-pity, cynicism – these are all forms of ill-will. They can all be dramatically curtailed through the practice of *metta* but ill-will, in whatever guise, is only finally overcome through the observation of transience.

Sloth & Torpor

Laziness in the meditation can manifest in one of two ways. The first type, sloth, occurs when the meditator doesn't want to apply himself to the practice. He feels comfortable and relaxed and prefers to sink into those pleasurable feelings rather than pay intelligent attention to the rise and fall. His mind drifts towards sleep. It may be pleasant enough but from the meditative perspective it is, of course, completely unproductive.

Paradoxically enough, the second type of laziness, torpor, is associated with too much effort.

Many new meditators, for example, erroneously believe that they should focus exclusively on the rise and fall of the abdomen. They try desperately to force the mind down on to this sensation, ignoring everything else in the process, including their craving to get on in the practice. This wrong use of effort results in torpor - the body becomes tense, the mind stiff and unwieldy, the practice seems joyless and claustrophobic.

This over-effortful approach is lazy because it's habitual. To many, trying too hard is so automatic that it is actually the easy option, it represents the line of least resistance.

To counteract sloth, the meditator needs to remind himself why he is meditating at all. He needs to remember that what he is trying to do is to come to understand everything about suffering and how it arises - which is infinitely more important than any pleasure gained from relaxing into drowsiness.

Actively investigating sensory experience can also help brighten the mind. When the mind is drowsy it wants to turn inwards, to withdraw - deliberately choosing to listen to sounds or to explore physical sensations reverses that trend.

If you try meditating straight after a meal, you'll find that the mind does tend to become sleepy. This natural physiological response is relatively short-lived. If you experience persistent sleepiness in the practice, it's more than likely that you're doing something wrong.

Sloth is not tiredness. If you've had a sleepless night or you've been doing a lot of physical work, you're going to feel tired. Meditatively, that's not a problem. The hindrance of sloth only arises when we identify with the feelings, when we stop trying to pay attention and surrender to the languor of semi-consciousness.

The critical factor in overcoming torpor is mindfulness. We have to see how we **choose** to apply too much effort in the moment. Until we break the habit of over-effort, we cannot apply ourselves intelligently.

In most cases over-effort is rooted in craving for progress. Such ambition can be deeply ingrained - ambition, after all, is actively encouraged in our culture. As well as mindfulness and restraint, the over-ambitious, goal-orientated meditator needs to develop such unselfish qualities as generosity and patience. By learning to divert his attention towards other people and away from himself, he will find that his mind tends automatically to adopt a more correct meditative perspective.

In the last analysis, the aim of the Buddhist path is to overcome all selfishness - a selfish approach to the path just doesn't work.

Worry & Restlessness

A man bought a brand-new car. He said to a friend who already owned the same model, 'Tell me what I need to worry about.'

Whenever there is worry in the mind, all we can think about is what might go wrong, what has gone wrong, what might have gone wrong and what is going wrong. In the absence of any obvious problem or concern, the worrying mind will simply manufacture problems.

Restlessness is a similarly agitated state. When someone is restless, he fidgets, he's distracted, he can't settle on anything.

When meditators are caught up in agitation, there are so many mental objects seeming to clamour for their attention - regretful thoughts, neurotic thoughts, anxieties, free associations, speculations - that they find it almost impossible to locate the sensation of the rise and fall. The volume of mental activity can seem overwhelming; the meditation session feels like it's lasting forever.

A surprisingly useful technique for countering worry is to deliberately put to one side, as it were, the specific concerns that are dominating the mind - financial problems, say. We can say to ourselves, 'The purpose of this hour is to help me come to understanding. I'll sort out what to do about my overdraft later.' Certainly, there are things in life that need planning but so much of what people would call planning is actually worry.

So often, we try to solve problems when we don't have all the necessary information. When paying meditative attention, concerns that are purely speculative – 'what might happen if' – are a complete waste of time.

To combat restlessness in meditation, it is essential to sit through the whole session. It may sound obvious but the first step in overcoming restlessness is sitting still.

The significant feature of a restless or worried mind is the absence of happiness. When we introduce happiness into the mind, restlessness and worry fall away. Just as we do hindrances, so can we do happiness. We can choose to think positively – we can think about everything that's right about our lives, for example, as opposed to what's wrong; we can call to mind what the Buddha said about enlightenment.

When this hindrance has been allayed, the mind stops jumping back into the past or forward into the future and is content to settle into the moment. Concerns that loomed large now seem insignificant; we wonder why we ever got so het up.

Doubt

A woman has become obsessed with her desire for a cigarette. She notes 'craving', tries to turn back to the rise and fall but in seconds flat the desire has arisen again. The craving seems so insistent that she's not sure how best to handle it.

Should she keep on trying to focus on the sensation in the abdomen? Or (recalling what she's heard about how to counter sense-desire) should she spend some time considering the disadvantages of smoking? She thinks about the health dangers of smoking - she turns back to the rise and fall ... She really can't decide which is the most effective approach; she fails to commit herself to either.

The fifth hindrance is doubt or wavering - essentially, oscillation between two or more possible courses of action.

A particularly pernicious form of this hindrance is doubt in the teaching itself. Some believe, for example, that what the Buddha said was fair enough for his own times but that some elements of the teaching - perhaps rebirth and other realms - are no longer relevant. Others believe that the observation of transience is too simple a practice to achieve real results.

Such doubts can plague the mind for weeks. With this kind of thinking going on - Should I try another path?

Does the teacher really understand my particular needs? Is there really such a thing as enlightenment? - application to the practice will be at best sporadic and half-hearted. And what makes this scepticism especially dangerous is that it can lead to people giving up the training altogether.

To a degree, doubts are inevitable - when we start out, we **don't** know whether the practice will work and we haven't had the experience to always know how best to apply ourselves.

For some, doubt is often a defence mechanism. Such people feel vulnerable because they don't have all the answers. If they could bring themselves to admit that they don't know, this would immediately weaken their attachment to their doubts.

But ultimately, there is only one way to put a stop to the potentially endless vacillations: make a decision and act on it.

For example, a new meditator might feel quite disturbed by the Buddha's teaching on non-self. Although he can just about see the logic of it intellectually, he resists it emotionally. He wastes most of his meditation sessions fretting over the problem.

His teacher points out that the only way he can resolve this impasse is by gaining some direct meditative experience. The teacher suggests that for a period of three months he consciously puts his doubts to one side and actually gets on with the practice. After three months, he will have far more **experience** of the teaching. The concept of *anatta* will be viewed from a very different perspective.

A fairly common type of doubt is doubt in one's own capacity to succeed in the meditation. Such doubts should simply be noted and put aside like any others. It should be remembered that the teaching is completely impersonal – ultimately, application to it will yield results, regardless of our expectations (negative or positive). If we apply ourselves properly, then suffering inevitably diminishes. Success in the teaching is solely dependent on following the eightfold path.

Politics, Therapy & Art

A man named Uttiya once asked if all the people in the world would realise enlightenment through the Buddha's teaching, or perhaps only a half or a third of them. One of the Buddha's closest disciples, Ananda, replied that the question was irrelevant. The Buddha was well aware that not everyone would be interested in the teaching. His sole concern was to make available the path to enlightenment.

Establishing a material utopia was never the Buddha's aim. He knew that, to a greater or lesser extent, human society would always contain corruption, inequality, oppression, political strife. He also knew that it was possible to go beyond worldly conditions altogether, and that he had the knowledge and skill to reveal the truth to those who wanted to see it.

The teaching is apolitical. Enlightenment is the raison d'être of everything the Buddha taught - introducing worldly concerns to the teaching only diverts attention from the real point of the path. An effective path to enlightenment, correctly taught, is a very rare thing. For a meditator to promote political or social ideals - however noble - above the quest for truth is to lose a valuable opportunity, an opportunity which may never come again.

Another side-track from the path is therapy. All unenlightened people could be said to be neurotic to some degree. All actions based in craving, hatred and ignorance are neurotic; if we hadn't craved, hated or ignored, we'd never have been born human in the first place. There are, of course, those whose neurosis is extreme - such people do need therapy or psychiatric help. Until their problems are overcome, trying to follow the path would be a waste of their time and could be counterproductive.

If someone is meditating correctly, it is inevitable that at times he will have to confront things about himself that he finds disturbing. If he can maintain a meditative perspective, he won't be unduly thrown by such revelations.

For example, it may suddenly become apparent to a meditator that the image of confidence he presents to the world is simply a mask, and that much of his behaviour is motivated by fear. Under the guidance of a competent instructor, he will learn to note the transience of the thoughts and feelings - the transience of the fear itself - and to restrain the strong temptation to identify with it all. Further, his teacher will stress the importance of regular *metta* practice, which cannot fail to start making him feel OK about himself.

The eightfold path the Buddha taught does not need augmenting - it is complete in itself. Those who wish to add therapy to the teaching may do so because they are confused about the goal of the path. Someone who has attained enlightenment may or may not be skilled at relating; he may or may not have a good relationship with his parents; he may or may not get tense in social gatherings. But he or she will never suffer.

One aspect of Buddhist culture that has received a lot of attention is art. Indeed, for some people, it is Buddhist art that provides the first point of contact with the teaching. But in the last analysis art - like therapy and politics - is a side-issue, something superfluous to the path to enlightenment.

There is no denying that the sight of a Buddha statue or a Thai temple may give tremendous pleasure. Indeed, the Buddhist tradition has produced some of the world's most sublime works of art. But no matter how intense and pleasurable the feelings, they **are** only feelings. No matter how inspired we might feel, inspiration does not preclude the need for meditative work. A beautiful object cannot do it for us.

The teaching is very subtle and easily corrupted. In every age, there are always side-issues which can be traps for the unwary. Whenever we get embroiled with these - and they can seem very alluring, even central to the meditative endeavour - we impose our own agenda and move away from the path laid down by the Buddha.

The Perfection of Giving

A Japanese monastery was getting very overcrowded. A merchant decided to donate five hundred pieces of gold towards the construction of a new building. He presented the money to the abbot who said, 'OK, I'll take it.'

The merchant was rather irritated by the teacher's response. 'Five hundred pieces of gold is a lot of money,' he remarked.

The teacher looked at him blankly. Then he said, 'Do you want me to thank you?'

'You should do.'

'Why should I? The giver should be grateful.'

The Buddhist attitude to giving is an aspect of the teaching which many westerners find challenging. The central idea that it is always the giver who benefits most was difficult enough for the Japanese merchant - for the average modern westerner, it goes right against the grain.

The Buddha placed great emphasis on the importance of generosity. 'Monks,' he once said, 'if beings knew, as I know, the result of giving and sharing, they would not eat without having given nor would they allow the stain of stinginess to obsess them and take root in their minds.

Even if it were their last morsel, their last mouthful, they would not enjoy eating without having shared it.'

While all acts of giving produce positive results, some acts are more positive than others. There are various criteria which determine the merit of a gift.

One is the attitude of the giver: the results of a gift given grudgingly are far inferior to those of one given wholeheartedly. If someone takes a proprietorial interest in what happens to a gift he's given, he has not truly given it. Someone who gives completely, without strings attached, is not concerned if the recipient passes the gift on to someone else or even throws it into the bin.

Another criterion is the value to the giver of the gift. Offloading things that are just cluttering up the house is a fairly tawdry form of giving. A true gift costs the giver, whether it's in terms of material resources or time.

A concept frequently encountered in Buddhism is 'fields of merit' - for westerners, this is perhaps one of the most alien aspects of the whole teaching. The Buddha taught that the mind of the recipient of a gift is a critical factor in the equation. The greater the development of wisdom and compassion in the recipient, the more positive the results to the giver.

Everyone has limited resources. Everyone makes a choice as to how much they wish to give and to whom they wish to give. Some give almost exclusively to their close family. Some give to refugees, addicts or victims of natural disaster. Others - more commonly those in the East - choose to give to those they believe embody the spiritual qualities to which they aspire.

In giving a gift, we are making a statement about our values. If we give only to our family, this suggests we believe the family to be the most important thing in life. If we give primarily to the disadvantaged, we believe perhaps that social justice is the highest good. In giving to those devoted to the quest for truth, we are indicating that following the path to enlightenment is our highest priority.

In giving a gift, a link is forged between the recipient and the giver. In giving to, say, a monk or nun, we are identifying with their aspirations and strengthening our commitment to those same goals.

Giving is in many ways a metaphor for the training itself. Essentially, we have to give up selfishness altogether and, in support of that end, the development of generosity is an invaluable aid.

The power of generosity should not be underestimated. But for the material support so freely given to monks and nuns and teachers of the path, past and present, the Buddha's teaching would not have survived.

Expressions of Compassion

Enlightenment is often described as the union of wisdom and compassion. Wisdom without compassion tends towards a cool insularity; compassion without wisdom tends towards sentimentality.

While meditation is indispensable, there is more to the spiritual path than the seated practice. It is no good spending hour after hour observing the three marks if, outside of the formal meditation, our lifestyle is predominantly selfish. For the practice to bear fruit, we must ensure that self-centredness is minimised. In short, we must develop compassion.

Compassion can be defined in terms of ten *parami* (or perfections), which include giving, *metta* and ethical conduct. All three are very obvious and direct ways of countering self-involvement. The other seven are renunciation, wisdom, energy, patience, truthfulness, determination and equanimity.

Renunciation is the refinement of ethical conduct, a subtler expression of restraint. Whereas the precepts deal solely with physical and verbal behaviour, renunciation includes mental restraint - letting go of attachment to a strongly-held opinion, for example.

Parenting will almost invariably provide countless opportunities for renunciation. There will be times when a mother is going to feel frustrated by the many demands that children inevitably make. At such times she has a choice. Either she becomes bitter and resentful, or she renounces her desire for time to herself.

In the context of the *parami*, wisdom refers specifically to wisdom about what is truly beneficial for beings. It is a common mistake to believe that compassion equates with always being nice. Compassion is the desire to alleviate pain and distress – letting people do what they want does **not** necessarily mean they will suffer less. You don't risk your child stumbling across pornography on the Internet, for example. In such cases, saying no is the most compassionate action.

The *parami* deal with compassion not only towards others but also towards oneself. An over-worked doctor, for example, has to have the wisdom to know when to stop. It's no good him working all hours and finding that his own health is collapsing.

The next *parami* is energy. It could be said that one of our major failings as human beings is that we are too easily seduced by security and comfort. Left to our own devices, we so often incline towards inertia. Developing this *parami* means consciously over-riding laziness. It means, for example, not simply switching off when a neighbour wants yet again to pour out her troubles, but actually listening.

Listening to a tedious neighbour also involves patience. The *parami* frequently overlap – so often a situation calls for the employment of a combination of different qualities.

Patience itself is closely allied to loving-kindness. Loving-kindness focuses on the positive qualities of beings – patience refuses to be offended by their negative qualities. We waste so much of our energy being offended by the actions of our fellow human beings. It is pointless to be annoyed by the hatred and craving in the world – hatred and craving are endemic and always will be.

The *parami* of truthfulness is traditionally expressed in terms of keeping promises. We only renege on a promise when keeping it is no longer convenient or advantageous to us – in other words, when self-interest takes precedence. Self-interest also motivates lying.

Some might say that there are occasions when untruths are justified – for example, telling a relative with a terminal illness that he's going to get better. The danger here is that we start playing God: we feel that it's up to us to decide whether someone can cope with the truth.

Truthfulness is of fundamental importance. The eightfold path is, after all, a path to truth. The more honest and straightforward we are in our dealings with the world, the more readily will we acknowledge and accept the truth of reality.

Compassion is not an easy option. If we set out to alleviate suffering in whatever form, we are bound to encounter obstacles – we have to be determined to see things through. If we fall at the first hurdle, the help we can provide is inevitably very limited. We have to be prepared to work with dedication for as long as it takes.

And are we going to get any thanks for what we do? This is where we come to the need for equanimity. If we expect the world to recognise our selfless actions, we are going to be disappointed. The need for appreciation subverts our efforts to get rid of selfishness. We train ourselves to practise compassion ideally without concern about recognition. When there is no attachment to results, there can be true compassion.

There is potentially no limit to the degree to which these *parami* could be cultivated. But to become enlightened, these qualities do not have to be developed to super-human levels - rather to the point where they counteract gross self-centredness in the mind, and thus allow the establishment of a correct meditative balance.

Compassion is the highest expression of selflessness in the world. Those who dedicate their life to helping others become a tremendous force for good in the world. As a result of their actions, they also gain inestimable benefits themselves.

But no matter how unselfish we train ourselves to be, we cannot become enlightened through compassion alone.

Psychic Powers

The monk Nanda was having a rough time. He told the Buddha that he wanted to leave the monkhood. The problem was, he was infatuated with a girl. When he had ordained, she had approached him 'with hair half-combed', whispering 'May you be back soon, young master.'

Through the exercise of his psychic powers, the Buddha took Nanda to one of the heaven realms and introduced him to some of the female devas. He later asked Nanda who was the more desirable – the human girl or the devas. Nanda replied that, compared to the devas, the girl looked like a mutilated monkey. 'Why, these devas are far lovelier, far more charming!' he enthused.

Later, a rumour went round the monastery that all Nanda was interested in was developing psychic powers so that he could get back to those female devas. The monks were very sarcastic to him.

Nanda felt humiliated and, in his shame, he started for the first time really to apply himself to the training. Apparently he soon made great progress.

The Buddha taught real men and women with real cravings and hatreds. He tailored his instructions according to the individual. His teaching methods could take surprising turns.

The Pali Canon (the collection of the Buddha's original teachings) describes many incidents involving psychic powers. The existence of such powers was accepted more or less without question by the culture of that day. Even though today we are generally more sceptical about such things, reports of out-of-the-body experiences and telepathy are commonplace.

Psychic phenomena are a reality – it is a natural function of mind to experience levels other than the gross material.

Buddhism defines several specific mental powers, all of which are developed through the exercise of concentration. They include experiencing past lives, mind-reading and the ability to travel in a mental body (what the West calls astral travelling).

During the course of their training, meditators sometimes have the occasional psychic experience – perhaps a fleeting glimpse of a previous existence – but that is quite different from having psychic powers. Only when we can exercise full conscious control – for example, recalling a past life or lives at will – can we be said to have a psychic power.

Developing psychic power needs a carefully controlled environment, frequent contact with a highly skilled and experienced instructor and, above all, a lot of time. Even with these optimum conditions, there is no guarantee of success.

Psychic powers are intriguing and seductive. Through the exercise of such powers, people can learn a great deal about the workings of the world. Someone who can look back into his past lives, for example, can gain great insight into why he is as he is today.

But psychic powers and the knowledge derived from them belong to the conventional level of truth, to the mundane world where beings are born, grow old and die. Psychic powers are mundane – they may be glamorous but they are still impermanent, unsatisfactory and non-self.

Some believe these powers to be a sign of great spiritual advancement. In Buddhism, however, they are seen as just another aspect of the wheel of birth and death, part of the up-market end of *samsara*.

For the *vipassana* meditator, the development of psychic powers constitutes a major detour. It is rare enough to encounter conditions favourable to meditative training and such conditions are at best precarious. Therefore most meditators would conclude that their time is better spent on the direct path to enlightenment.

The Recollections

A Tibetan teacher once remarked on how strange and surprising he found the average westerner's low sense of self-esteem. This is undoubtedly a major area of difficulty for western meditators.

The regular practice of loving-kindness meditation is the most effective method of improving the way we feel about ourselves. Another invaluable technique is the practice of what are known as the recollections.

As with *metta*, systematic development of the recollections introduces a positive bias to the mind. A mind filled with hindrances sees everything through the filter of self-concern and is incapable of paying meditative attention. Practising the recollections entails consciously thinking about positive aspects of the path in order to brighten the mind.

There are times when the mind seems to get locked into negativity. Rather than laboriously trying to force the mind on to the rise and fall, what the meditator should do is deliberately change tack. He needs to do something which in *vipassana* meditation we usually try to restrain - he needs to start thinking.

He might start thinking about the qualities of the Buddha. He spends some time considering examples of the

Buddha's compassion, his skill in teaching, his insight into human nature, with the result that the whole tone of the mind is transformed. Self-involvement is supplanted by interest and enthusiasm. Once he has established a more meditative mind-set, he turns the mind once again to the observation of transience.

Thinking about the Dhamma, the teaching itself, or about those people, past and present, who have themselves followed in the Buddha's footsteps produces a similar effect. Another traditional subject for recollection is one's own ethical behaviour. To remember that one has kept the precepts for some time can help introduce a more accurate perspective into a mind plagued by self-doubt, for example.

For those inclined to indulge in self-pity or envy, recollecting their own good fortune can have a dramatic effect on the mind. It is easy to forget that for so many beings violence, poverty, hunger loom large.

It can be difficult initially to get a recollection going – inertia is a major component of self-indulgence; thinking positive thoughts can be the last thing we want to do. Having seen through experience, however, how effective the recollections can be, we are much more inclined to put them into practice.

Vipassana meditation is not about thinking. There are times, though, when the mind is riddled with thinking anyway – thoughts of me, what I want and what I'm not getting. It is then that the meditator should use the recollections – introducing specific trains of thought which balance the mind and allow a return to the observation of transience. He thinks to overcome thinking.

Retreats

Meditation only works when practised daily. Like any other skill, the more of it you do, the better you get. However, our tendency to ignore is not easily overcome. Even with an hour or two's seated practice each day and the attempt to be systematically mindful, we can still have blind-spots; because of these areas of ignorance, freedom still eludes us.

For most people, the way forward is to spend regular periods of time practising intensively. Typically, this might involve a couple of weeks a year on formal retreat.

In a retreat setting, there is nothing to do but develop mindfulness and concentration. If the retreat is properly set up, distractions are minimised – there is no talking, no entertainment, no newspapers or television – nothing to take the mind away from the task in hand. Such a situation is ideally suited to the development of mindfulness.

To get the most out of a retreat, it makes sense to approach it in the right way. This might entail cutting down on social activities beforehand and tying up loose ends such as unpaid bills, so one doesn't subsequently waste time worrying. The idea is to embark on a retreat in as meditative and undistracted a frame of mind as possible.

The best retreat environment is one that is neither too luxurious nor too ascetic, nor particularly exotic. If someone travels to, say, India to attend a retreat, the chances are that the adjustment to a foreign culture will so distract him that he never really gets down to the work of meditation. The conditions of a retreat should ideally contain as little as possible to stimulate the mind. Indeed, in many respects, they should be boring.

From a meditative perspective, boredom is an interesting phenomenon. Our normal response to it is escape – we pick up the phone or turn on the television. It is really only on a retreat that we have the chance to actually confront boredom and find out exactly what it is. Only when we know what it is do we have the opportunity to overcome it.

Of pivotal importance to the success of a retreat is skilled instruction. Without the guidance of an experienced teacher, the meditator is inevitably going to waste a lot of time – subtly or not so subtly – misdirecting his efforts. A teacher can suggest new lines of enquiry; he can encourage and inspire; he can prompt us to look at things we'd rather not. He or she can also prod us if we get complacent.

However, even if we find the best teacher and the most conducive retreat environment, it is still up to us to make the most of this good fortune. Nothing and no one can do the work for us.

Happiness

King Pasenadi once said that, in contrast to the monks of other traditions, the Buddha's monks always looked 'very joyful, very exultant, contented and cheerful'.

The arising of happiness is a natural and inevitable consequence of following the path. It is a subtler form of happiness than that derived from sense-pleasures, career or material possessions. It is also more stable than any kind of worldly happiness, because it is far less dependent on the vagaries of external circumstances.

For example, the happiness that comes from living by the precepts is quite different from the happiness that comes from, say, indulging in gossip. Wrong speech may well be enjoyable enough at the time but it always leads to us feeling bad about ourselves.

Worldly happiness is excited, brittle, restless. There is often a tinge of anxiety accompanying it - how long can we make it last?

For many, discovering a teaching which makes sense of life and which promises a complete end to all searching brings a tremendous sense of relief. There is at last the prospect of a happiness that endures, a happiness that transcends the relentless cycles of holiday and work, marriage and divorce, birth and death.

The more mindful we become, the more we learn to enjoy things for their own sake, rather than for what we can get out of them. The more insight we gain into the mark of non-self and the more we see that self is nothing but a fleeting idea, the less seriously we can take ourselves. And rather than always looking out for self-advantage, we can even begin to laugh at ourselves.

Not only does happiness develop as a result of correctly following the path - it is itself an essential component of successful practice. A mind that is settled, contented, cheerful, concentrates far more readily. When concentration is present, mindfulness is more easily cultivated.

Simply, a happy mind is much better suited to the practice of meditation. Practising the recollections and *metta* helps allay negative mental states and produces happiness. This happiness itself advances our efforts along the path.

The conclusion of the path the Buddha described as the highest happiness. This is not happiness in the worldly sense - rather it is the happiness of freedom, the happiness of non-attachment.

Conceit

The purpose of the training is to overcome selfishness, self-importance, self-concern – each and every aspect of self-view. It is no surprise then that one of the most insidious obstacles to progress is conceit. Everyone knows how distasteful and unpleasant it is to be around people who are full of themselves. Consider as an example an academic who prides himself on his intellect and lack of interest in the material world – he radiates a smug self-satisfaction.

In Buddhism, the term 'conceit' describes not only this type of overbearing superiority but also what are known as inferiority and equality conceits.

It is culturally acceptable to believe that there is nothing wrong with doing yourself down, always focusing on your faults – in fact there is even a tendency to see this as a virtue. The Buddha taught that believing yourself to be the worst is just as bad as believing yourself to be the best.

The woman who insists on seeing herself as, say, the worst mother in the neighbourhood is obsessed with herself in relation to other mothers. Her thoughts revolve around herself, her shortcomings, her failures. Her envy, anxiety and constant comparisons make her very difficult to be around. She is just as self-centred as the mother who thinks she's perfect.

The third type of conceit, the equality conceit, is more subtle yet. In Buddhist terms, the person who believes that he is just as good – or just as bad – as another is conceited. Whenever we are attached to **any** thoughts of me or myself, we are conceited.

Self only exists as an idea. In reality, there are just transient moments of mental and physical experience – there is nothing that continues on, no controlling entity, no fixity. To identify with, to become attached to, the concept of self (or indeed any other idea) is to court disaster. The academic who identifies himself as a person who has gone beyond concern with material possessions succeeds only in isolating himself and alienating others.

The idea of self, an independent agent separated out from the flow of phenomena, runs counter to reality – in reality there are no selves. The idea of self is real enough and the results of our attachment to it are real enough. In short, it produces suffering.

It is easy to fall into the trap of thinking that comparison itself is the problem, that any comparison of myself with another inevitably involves conceit. But the real problem is attachment and it is quite possible to make comparisons without attachment in the mind.

For example, it is fair enough to say that a man with a string of degrees is more intellectually accomplished than someone who couldn't get through their school exams. Similarly, if you are interviewing candidates for a job, you **have** to evaluate their qualifications and skills. We all inevitably spend a lot of time making these kinds of decisions, assessing and comparing.

Problems arise when people confuse such assessments with value judgements. An assessment is simply a cool, functional appraisal of suitability (which may or may not be accurate). A value judgement on the other hand is passionate, prejudiced and self-involved. If we believe that someone not suitable for the job is somehow inferior as a human being, then we are guilty of conceit.

Sometimes people shy away from their gut instinct about an individual or a situation. They overlay their true feelings with a veneer of apologetic politeness, fearing that their judgement will be construed as conceit. Such evasion is counterproductive for the meditator, who is training himself to see the truth of all things as they are.

Sex

Contrary to what some people have believed – and sometimes have believed very strongly – both men and women can and do become enlightened. The path is effective for anyone who follows it, irrespective of race, age, background or gender. However, if conceit arises because of attachment to, say, gender, progress is not possible.

Every mind has masculine aspects and feminine aspects. Every meditator has to acknowledge and accept **all** aspects of mind. So anyone who believes that one gender is superior to the other has got a problem.

A man who denigrates women will also undervalue and ignore his own feminine qualities. He will find loving-kindness meditation hard-going. He will also find it difficult to give a personal gift to his teacher, although he might have little trouble giving anonymously.

A woman who holds masculinity in low esteem won't see the point in sitting through an hour of meditation if the practice is painful. She will also struggle to recognise that there are occasions when the most compassionate action is to leave someone alone.

It is also, of course, possible for men to hate their masculinity and women their femininity. As far as the meditator is concerned, all such chauvinism has to be overcome.

The Buddha stated quite categorically that, of all possible sense-objects, none is so alluring as the sight, sound and touch of a member of the opposite sex. It is hardly surprising then that meditators can sometimes be thrown by the intensity of their craving for sex. This is partly due to the influence of our Judaeo-Christian conditioning, which tends to equate sexuality with immorality.

From a Buddhist point of view, craving for sex is essentially no different from any other kind of craving. It is the craving that's the problem – not sex per se. The meditator comes to recognise that the desire for sex, like all other desires, is conditioned and, crucially, transient.

Craving is not a prerequisite for sex – celibacy is not a prerequisite for enlightenment. The enlightened person may or may not have a sexual relationship but he or she does not crave for sex nor for anything else.

Death

As soon as King Pukkusati heard about the Buddha and his teaching, he gave up his throne and set off to find him. Arriving in the town of Rajagaha, he arranged to spend the night in a potter's shed. He and another man who'd also asked for lodging there spent the night in meditation.

In the early hours of the morning, Pukkusati's companion started talking about the path to enlightenment. He spoke with such assurance and such authority that it suddenly dawned on Pukkusati that this was the man he'd set out to find. He immediately asked the Buddha if he could become a monk. The Buddha agreed. But within hours Pukkusati was dead, gored by a cow.

Death can come at any time (even when you've just come across the teaching).

The Buddhist attitude to death is diametrically opposed to that of modern western society. Rather than pretending it will never happen, the meditator actually uses the fact of death as a source of motivation. If for example a close relative dies, rather than avoiding the sight of a corpse at all costs, the meditator will not shy away from viewing the dead body.

As long as we ignore death, we live irresponsibly. We believe we have endless time to indulge our trivial desires and anxieties. Confronting the reality of death is the most effective way of ordering our priorities. When we remember that death can come at any moment, we don't waste time.

Because death does provide such a spur, there has evolved in the Buddhist tradition a set of formal recollections on the subject. Whenever the meditator is feeling lazy or complacent, a recollection on death will help enthuse the mind. It is also a very powerful counter for sense-desire, especially for lust.

For example, you might think about the fact that nothing - the greatest fame, the greatest riches, the greatest power, the greatest wisdom - nothing stops people dying - Frank Sinatra, Kublai Khan, the Buddha himself ...

Alternatively, you might reflect on how precarious your existence is. At any moment, a group of cells might turn cancerous, a blood vessel in your brain might haemorrhage, the brakes on your car might fail.

None of us knows when our last moment will come.

Much has been written about the way this final moment of consciousness conditions the following lifetime. The death moment is significant but it is itself conditioned by what came before. Basically, if our attempts to follow the path have been half-hearted, by then it's too late.

The enlightened person has broken free from the wheel of birth and death, and there has been a great deal of speculation about what happens to such people after the death of the physical body.

The Buddha would not answer this question. With enlightenment the idea of self, of a solid enduring personality, can never again arise. How then can one talk in terms of a person who is born and dies?

Progress

It is not surprising that the new meditator, reading about the path to enlightenment, often wonders about how much progress he's made, not to speak of when (or if) he's going to get enlightened.

People can have strange ideas about what constitutes meditative progress. Some equate progress simply with the ability to concentrate, with seeing discs of light in the mind or experiencing intensely pleasurable feelings. Others see meditation as giving them the ability to control their minds; they may try to convince themselves – and others – that they are 'equanimous to everything', they don't experience emotions any more.

Progress can be defined simply as a growing experiential understanding of the fact that everything is transient, unsatisfactory and non-self. The more insight we have into these three marks, the less we suffer.

Meditators who are practising correctly will find that they're not so bothered by the vicissitudes of life. Knowing that nothing lasts, they don't get so thrown by either failures or successes. They might still get irritable or despondent but these moods last for minutes rather than hours or days. They become less defensive, less concerned with self-image, more open.

One early sign of progress for some meditators is, paradoxically enough, the feeling that they're getting worse. They think they're getting more anxious, more passionate, more intolerant, when in fact all that's happening is that they are becoming more aware. For the first time they are clearly seeing what has always been there. And it is only when we do see what's there that we have any chance of doing something about it.

Self-assessment is not always easy. We can be too involved to have the objectivity necessary to make an accurate judgement. If, however, a meditator looks back after, say, six months or a year of practice, he will clearly recognise the changes that have taken place.

One stage on the path that all meditators must pass through is traditionally referred to as 'overcoming elation and depression'. In the early days, we tend to get over-excited when we think the practice is going well and depressed when we think it's not.

Over the weeks and months, we gradually come to recognise that these mood swings are a waste of time and energy - all they do is take us away from the task of paying attention. As mindfulness strengthens, we learn to include in the meditation our emotional responses to the practice itself.

As insight into transience develops, the meditation naturally progresses through different stages. At some points, the practice seems to unfold effortlessly; at others its tone is characterised by fear, for example, or by an overwhelming desire to be free of suffering.

None of these things need cause any problem - they are the inevitable outcome of paying attention to transience. Wherever we are on the path, the practice is the same. Irrespective of which stage we're at (or which stage we think we're at), all we need to do is continue observing the rise and fall of all things.

If we're practising correctly, insight will arise - progress is inevitable. If we could accept this, there would be no problem. But for many meditators there **is** a problem, because they want insight now. The craving for progress is a serious meditative obstacle. It leads to over-effort, disenchantment, anxiety, doubt. When we are obsessed with progress or forever looking for signs of it, we cannot be paying attention to the mark of transience.

To make progress, we have to become aware of our craving for progress. We have to stop grasping at expectations, ambition, ideas about progress.

No one can predict when insight will arise, when a meditator will become enlightened. No one knows how much work we have already done in previous lives.

Progress is not linear - sometimes everything seems to fall into place; sometimes we seem to be going round in circles. But, ultimately, whether the practice is enjoyable or difficult is of no real consequence. Chasing pleasure, avoiding pain is the way of the world; it is *samsara*. As long as we are not enlightened, we still need to keep watching transience.

Stream-winning

There is a point on the path at which enlightenment is assured. This is traditionally known as stream-winning, the stage at which the meditator 'enters the stream' that leads irrevocably to *nibbana*. It is said that those who reach this stage can never again be reborn in lower realms and have at most only seven more lifetimes before they become enlightened.

At the moment of stream-winning, the meditator has a glimpse of *nibbana*. For the first time, the mind stops grasping at the world and, for a moment, takes *nibbana* as its object.

Having seen *nibbana*, doubt is no longer possible. The meditator now knows where he's going and he knows (more or less) how to get there. He knows for a fact that the way to enlightenment is the development of the eightfold path. He knows he's got to do the work himself. Never again can he be tempted by the idea of a spiritual shortcut, whether it's through crystals, diet, healing or discarnate spirit guides.

Glimpsing *nibbana* also seriously undermines the meditator's belief in self. The view of self, however, runs deep and, to destroy it completely, more work is required.

Stream-winning is in many senses the most significant event in the meditator's training. Now he cannot fall back – freedom is guaranteed.

Why Follow The Path

In the world, there is an infinite number of different avenues we could choose to explore. There is an infinite number of skills we could learn, an infinite number of lifestyles and roles we could experiment with. The world is alluring - it seems to offer so much. We can spend a long, long time exploring.

But for each of us the realisation gradually dawns that pleasure cannot exist without pain, that relationships form only to dissolve, that there cannot be birth without death. No matter how successful and powerful someone may become, scratch the surface and you find the seeds of alienation, restlessness, frustration, insecurity.

Samsara is the realm of broken dreams.

There is, however, a beyond.

On a night of the full moon, a group of monks was sitting together in the sal-wood at Gosinga. Sariputta, one of the Buddha's chief disciples, posed a question. He asked what kind of monk would best illumine the forest grove, with the sal-trees in full blossom and 'deva-like scents wafted around'.

Many different answers were put forward. One monk praised those with an extensive knowledge of the teaching.

Another said that he found those with psychic powers most impressive. Another said that the kind of person who would best complement this idyllic setting was one with flawless self-discipline. Sariputta himself felt that a monk with exquisite mental control was most praiseworthy.

Today, things aren't so different. Some might say that the ideal Buddhist is one who is politically engaged and who champions the cause of the oppressed. Others value above all else intellectual understanding. Others still are most impressed by those who represent the ancient unbroken lineages of the East.

The monks in the forest grove went to see the Buddha and Sariputta told him about their discussion. The Buddha then gave his own answer to the question. He said that the best monk is one who meditates determined that he will never give up, until the day he becomes enlightened.

★ ★ ★

In an age of extravagant claims and hyperbole, the Buddha's description of enlightenment - 'the end of suffering' - might at first seem understated. But think what that really means.

The enlightened person no longer thinks in terms of life being all right when ... He no longer believes that life would be all right if ... He no longer puts off his life.

Only the enlightened person has truly abandoned all those thoughts and feelings about life not really being good enough. Only the enlightened person knows that things are perfect as they are.

Other books available from Aukana

A MEDITATION RETREAT

Alan & Jacqui James

The Buddha said that there is just one way to overcome the suffering seemingly inherent in the human condition. The practice of mindfulness generates insight into the way our minds work, revealing why it is that we feel dissatisfied and distressed, and exactly how suffering can be overcome.

With a clarity and directness of approach that can only come from understanding, Alan and Jacqui James elucidate the practice of mindfulness, covering such topics as how to meditate, hindrances to the practice and how to surmount them, the relationship between teacher and student—and enlightenment itself, the final goal of the spiritual journey.

Based on profound experience and very clearly written ... there is much throughout the book which will prove of benefit to many - **The Middle Way**

A very informative book about the nature of the practice ... of benefit to both beginners and more experienced meditators - **Visuddhacara Bhikkhu,** *author of* Curbing Anger, Spreading Love

ISBN 0-9511769-0-0   *216 x 138mm   224 pages*

MODERN BUDDHISM

Alan & Jacqui James

'The Buddha's teaching is as relevant today as it ever has been. It describes the facts of human life which are observable by anyone who cares to take the trouble to investigate.'

Presenting timeless truths in a 20th-century context, *Modern Buddhism* provides answers to questions that have always haunted mankind.

Death and dying: a wasted and terrifying experience—or an opportunity for spiritual growth? A meditation teacher describes the way she helped her mother approach the doors of death.

Family relationships: why do some families live in harmony, whilst others are constantly at war? What is the purpose of the family unit?

Sexuality: what sexual habits are most conducive to progress along the path?

Alan and Jacqui James belong to the tradition of teachers who present the essence of Buddhism in a way which is totally in tune with the needs of their own time and culture.

In a confused and dark world, the book is like a ray of light showing the path to sanity and peace - **Buddhism Today, Brisbane**

ISBN 0-9511769-1-9   *215 x 135mm   176 pages*

INNER TRANQUILLITY
The Buddha's Path to Freedom

Alan James

*'The successful spiritual traveller completely understands suffering.
He knows through experience its conditioned nature, its origins and
its cessation. Having won to the deathless, he knows with a
knowing that goes beyond words that he is free—that the universe
is love—that the journey is ended—there is no more to do. He is
finally at peace.'*

Inner tranquillity is a universal goal.

Inner tranquillity, it could be argued, is *the* universal goal, the
goal of all existence, however various our attempts to reach it.

The Buddha uncovered a systematic, comprehensive and—
most importantly—effective pathway to the attaining of that
which all of us seek.

In this collection of lectures, Alan James draws on over thirty
years of teaching experience to illuminate this path to the
ultimate peace.

*There is much that is wise and helpful here ... a detailed and useful
guide to meditation -* **Buddhism Now**

*Written with a down-to-earth tone ... James gives lots of practical
advice ... from the perspective of someone who has travelled the path -*
Living Traditions, Australia

*One of the best books on the teaching of the Buddha, written by a
person of great learning ... in lucid simple language and in a clear
style -* **Buddhist Publication Society Newsletter**

ISBN 0-9511769-8-6   *234 x 156mm   224 pages*

THE UNFOLDING OF WISDOM
The Buddha's Path to Enlightenment

Alan James

' ... *it is like having lived all your life in a dark cave, never being sure where the walls, the ceiling or the exits were, never being sure of the real shape of the space around you. When at last you bring in some light to the darkness, immediately your old idea of the cave disappears. The illumination of true vision eliminates what had been total darkness, including all your speculations about the reality of the cave.*

'When this occurs, there is never any need to refer to your earlier idea of how things were; it simply becomes irrelevant. Now you know things as they are. What interest can speculative fantasies have for you now?'

The Unfolding of Wisdom is uncompromising. It presents the facts about spiritual progress. It is not for those who would speculate about symbolism or metaphor but for those who would dare to approach truth directly.

ISBN 0-9511769-4-3 (hardback)   *240 x 165mm   224 pages*
     0-9511769-5-1 (softback)   *230 x 155mm   224 pages*

BUDDHISM IN A FOREIGN LAND

Robert Mann

As Buddhism is taking root in the West, evolving new forms to suit new conditions, much of its traditional oriental context is being called into question.

In this intriguing and provocative collection of talks, Robert Mann addresses many of the issues which confront Buddhism as it adapts to modern western culture.

Rebirth and traditional cosmology, the role of ethics in a global consumer society, the dangers inherent in confusing therapy with spirituality—these are just some of the topics included in this controversial book.

Covers in an admirably clear manner the fundamentals of the Buddhadharma ... a book to be recommended - **Journal of Buddhist Ethics**

A pleasure to read—lucid, unambiguous and expressive - **Buddhism Now**

ISBN 0-9511769-6-X   *215 x 135mm   192 pages*

BUDDHIST CHARACTER ANALYSIS

Robert Mann & Rose Youd

Food, sleep, relationships, sex: do you go for quality, quantity or moderation? Or would you prefer to live without them?

Buddhist Character Analysis is a practical guide to the infinite complexities of human behaviour.

You're offered your own TV show. Do you think, 'What took them so long?' Or would you rather die?

Based exclusively on observable facts, **Buddhist Character Analysis** identifies our fundamental motives and assumptions.

Does your heart sink at the prospect of a quiet weekend? Or do you believe that the world could be a wonderful place if it wasn't for all those people?

Skilful use of **Buddhist Character Analysis** leads to a greater understanding of human nature and increasing happiness in daily life.

How do you see the enlightened person? An aloof Himalayan hermit, master of self-control? Or a charismatic leader using his powers to create a better world?

Combined with a spiritual training, **Buddhist Character Analysis** deepens insight into the true nature of reality.

A thoroughly readable introduction to the subject - **Holistic London Guide**

ISBN 0-9511769-3-5   *197 x 123mm   144 pages*

LIFE AS A SIAMESE MONK

Richard Randall

May 1954, Bangkok—10,000 people converge on the outlying temple of Wat Paknam to witness an historic ceremony. 47-year-old journalist Richard Randall is taking the saffron robe to ordain as a Buddhist monk. Known henceforth as Kapilavaddho Bhikkhu, he is the first Englishman to enter the monkhood in Thailand. After an intensive meditation training and some remarkable experiences in concentration and insight practice, Kapilavaddho later went on to play a key role in the introduction of Buddhist meditation to the West.

An exceptionally fine Dhamma-read - **Buddhism Now**

An inspiring story of Buddhist devotion - **Light of Peace, Bangkok**

ISBN 0-9511769-2-7
230 x 150mm   224 pages + 8 pages b/w photographs

These books are available by mail-order:

Buddhism: The Plain Facts	£6.95
A Meditation Retreat	£7.95
Modern Buddhism	£7.95
Inner Tranquillity	£8.95
The Unfolding of Wisdom	
softback	£8.95
hardback	£10.95
Buddhism in a Foreign Land	£8.50
Buddhist Character Analysis	£6.95
Life as a Siamese Monk	£8.95

Prices include postage and packing

Please send to:

Aukana Trust
9 Masons Lane
Bradford on Avon
Wiltshire
BA15 1QN
England

e-mail: info@aukana.org.uk
www.aukana.org.uk
Telephone: (01225) 866821
International: +44 1225 866821